Ghosts of

Other titles in this series include:

GHOSTS OF BERKSHIRE
Ian McLoughlin

DERBYSHIRE GHOSTS & LEGENDS
David Bell

GHOSTS OF EAST ANGLIA
Harold Mills-West

GHOSTS OF HERTFORDSHIRE
Betty Puttick

LEICESTERSHIRE GHOSTS & LEGENDS
David Bell

GHOSTS & LEGENDS OF LINCOLNSHIRE &
THE FEN COUNTRY
Polly Howat

NORFOLK GHOSTS & LEGENDS
Polly Howat

NORTHAMPTONSHIRE GHOSTS & LEGENDS
Marian Pipe

GHOSTS & LEGENDS OF STAFFORDSHIRE &
THE BLACK COUNTRY
David Bell

GHOSTS OF SURREY
John Janaway

SUSSEX GHOSTS AND LEGENDS
Tony Wales

GHOSTS OF WARWICKSHIRE
Betty Smith

Ghosts
of
Buckinghamshire

Betty Puttick

COUNTRYSIDE BOOKS
NEWBURY, BERKSHIRE

Countryside Books
3 Catherine Road
Newbury, Berkshire

ISBN 1 85306 324 X

Cover illustration by Colin Doggett

Produced through MRM Associates Ltd., Reading
Typeset by Paragon Typesetters, Clwyd
Printed by J.W. Arrowsmith Ltd., Bristol

To my children, and their children,
with much love

Contents

Acknowledgements

My grateful thanks to all the people who so kindly helped me with my enquiries, especially Desmond Bonner, Wesley Downes, Mr Georgiou, Patricia Hillier, Elizabeth Knight, Alastair MacLeod Matthews, Judy Tipping and Elizabeth Wiltshire.

Ghosts
of
Buckinghamshire

N

Olney

Newport
Pagnell

Stony
Stratford

Passenham

Woughton
on the Green

Bletchley

BUCKINGHAM

Newton
Longville

Soulbury

Middle
Clayton

Stewkley

AYLESBURY VALE

AYLESBURY

Haddenham

Chesham

Great
Missenden

Amersham

Chenies
Manor

CHILTERNS

Hughenden

West
Wycombe

HIGH
WYCOMBE

Turville

Fingest

Beaconsfield

Chalfont
St Peter

Skirmett

Gerrards
Cross

Hambleden

Farnham
Common

Medmenham
Abbey

Colnbrook

OLNEY

NEWPORT PAGNELL

THREE LOCKS,
SOULBURY

BUCKINGHAM

FINGEST

AMERSHAM

HIGH WYCOMBE

Introduction

'TALKING of ghosts,' said Samuel Johnson, 'It is wonderful that five thousand years have now elapsed since the creation of the world, and still it is undecided whether or not there has ever been an instance of the spirit of any person appearing after death. All argument is against it; but all belief is for it.'

How true. People still ask someone like me 'Have you ever seen a ghost?' rather as if they were asking if I had ever encountered a dinosaur. And others will recount some remarkable paranormal experience, adding 'Of course, I'm a sceptic', lest they should be written off as some kind of crackpot.

But most of us enjoy a good ghost story, and if it's true, so much the better. Buckinghamshire has proved to have an interesting supply of many different aspects of the paranormal. There are apparitions of the famous, like Charles I's standard bearer, Edmund Verney, still haunting Claydon House after 350 years, and Disraeli at his beloved Hughenden, even a disembodied Henry VIII at Chenies.

But ghosts do not confine themselves to stately homes, they are just as likely to move in on the occupants of a council house or a cottage, as I discovered.

Pubs, restaurants and cinemas, phone boxes and railway stations are as prone to haunting as the Tower of London. Perhaps you, too, have heard footsteps approaching, but no one walks by? Or you notice a lady in a crinoline, or a man in a Cavalier's cloak and feathered hat – must be a fancy dress party somewhere, you think – and then they walk

9

through the wall!

In Buckinghamshire, there are roads where Dick Turpin still lies in wait for the unwary traveller, where a coach and horses or a solitary rider may thunder by in the moonlight, or a spectral jaywalker throw himself unexpectedly in front of your wheels. And beware the black dog with the eyes like coach lamps that may pad along behind you as you walk home late one night. It may just be some stray labrador out for a bedtime stroll – or it may be the hound from hell.

People who state with pride that they do not believe in ghosts have usually had no contact with the paranormal. And yet, experiences such as I describe in this book are happening every day to people like you and me. Some are quite subtle, a sudden unexpected chill in the air, a cold spot in an otherwise warm room, or the scent of violets or jasmine on a winter's day. But all, like the foot on the stairs in an empty house, are a sign that there are more things in heaven and earth than are dreamt of by doubting Horatios.

I have been a journalist for many years and I have simply reported the stories I have found, and I know there must be many more.

My book on the *Ghosts of Hertfordshire* was published in October 1994, and since then I have heard from people who have also experienced some of the hauntings I described. Others had new stories that I was interested to hear. Maybe it will happen again with *Ghosts of Buckinghamshire*? I hope so.

Betty Puttick
Autumn 1995

Haunted Missenden

TODAY, picturesque Missenden Abbey is an Adult Education College and little is left of the original building, an ancient abbey founded by Augustinian monks in 1133.

The doubtful activities of the infamous Black Monks of Missenden might have been expected to leave some paranormal happenings behind. Indeed, as Hippisley Coxe says in his book *Haunted Britain*, in 1530 a monk should not have been seen coming out of a house in the village dressed in doublet and jerkin with a sword by his side! And yet the phantom most frequently reported has been a lady in a crinoline, seen on the main staircase.

Two students sitting reading one day near this staircase were startled to see a figure floating down the stairs and out through the door, and by her old fashioned style of dress and general appearance, they were convinced that she was not of this world. In the summer of 1972, another student reported seeing a similar figure near one of the ladies' cloakrooms, where sightings of the same phantom had previously been reported. The only query is regarding the crinoline the ghost is wearing. Sometimes it is described as grey, sometimes white or even black.

Some of the ghost's behaviour could be described as rather unseemly for a Victorian lady, however. On one occasion a flower vase was thrown down the staircase, and in the 1970s a heavy glass ashtray was found smashed in pieces in a student's bedroom, both events which at the time were ascribed to the crinoline-wearer.

Staff working late in the building have heard an eerie wailing cry echoing down the corridors, and once in the winter after a heavy fall of snow, a security guard was baffled to find footsteps which started and finished in the middle of nowhere!

About half a mile away from Missenden Abbey is Little Abbey Hotel, originally a convent for nuns in the 12th century. It is said to have been connected to Missenden Abbey by a secret passage, used by monks to visit the convent supposedly to administer the sacraments to the nuns, but the notoriety of the monks' often scandalous behaviour suggests that they may have had other plans.

At one period the Little Abbey Hotel was used as a preparatory school and it was during this time that a passage leading to the abbey was discovered. The entrance was through a trapdoor in what had been the ballroom, and it was blocked up and cemented over.

By 1297, there seems to have been an attempt to tighten up discipline at the abbey, as one young novice found to his cost when he was caught in a compromising situation with a nun from the nearby convent. Fearing the consequences, he is said to have cut his own throat and it is thought to be his monk-like apparition which haunts the hotel to this day, and ghostly echoes of his terrible end have been heard from a room by the minstrels' gallery overlooking the dining room.

One day the hotel handyman was on the staircase landing, doing some repair work to a window, when he saw a figure in a brown hooded cloak coming up the stairs. 'He had his hands together as if in prayer,' he said, 'and as he passed me I wished him "Good morning" and turned back to my work.'

But after a time, when this rather oddly dressed visitor did not return, the handyman decided to check as there was only a toilet on the top floor, the other rooms used by staff being locked. He found all the doors locked as usual, and no sign of the man who had passed him, and the staff were of the opinion that the monk's ghost, which had been quite active in the hotel in previous years, had made a reappearance.

Missenden had another ghost in Hugh de Plesseter, Lord of Missenden, who died in 1292. He had left inconvenient instructions that he should be buried before the high altar in Missenden Abbey, seated on his white palfrey, Principall!

The monks were not pleased by this unusual and eccentric request, but they dared not refuse, and his wishes were carried out. But even so, on dark and stormy nights when the wind howled through the valley, the fearsome ghost of Hugh de Plesseter came thundering by on his war horse, and local citizens knew that this was no time to be abroad if you valued your life!

This story bears an uncanny resemblance to the strange history of one Captain Backhouse (see *Gentlemen (and Ladies) of the Road* chapter), who had equally original ideas about his burial, and was just as troublesome afterwards.

A Couple of Bogeymen

'BEHAVE yourself, or wicked Bobby Banistre will come and get you.'

Many a child must have heard this dire threat in times gone by, and even grown-ups were known to shiver in their shoes at the prospect of encountering the ghost of a man whose evil and oppressive reputation in life and spine-chilling activities after death were not easy to forget.

Sir Robert Bannistre was Lord of the Manor of Passenham, near Stony Stratford. He was a great man in his day, being Comptroller of the Household of King James I and Court Victualler to King Charles I. His striking memorial is in St Guthlac's church at Passenham, but the memories he left behind with the people who had experienced his harsh and ruthless behaviour were such that his death was a cause for general celebration in the locality.

The widespread relief at the end of a cruel, hated tyrant was, however, short-lived. The word soon spread that, although Sir Robert was undoubtedly no longer in the land of the living, his armour-clad spectre had been seen striding through the country lanes, and had even appeared by the bedsides of some of his terrified tenants.

Even worse, as the sexton was digging his grave, his unmistakable ghostly apparition appeared alongside, and in fearful tones laden with doom uttered the words 'I am not yet ready.' Not surprisingly, the sexton almost died on the spot himself.

However, the burial service eventually went ahead, but as the coffin was lowered into the grave, yet again those assembled at the graveside heard a chilling, sepulchral voice cry out 'I am not yet ready.'

Ready or not, Sir Robert was buried, but his ghostly activities continued unabated in the area, and were so alarming that a service of exorcism was arranged. But, before it was finished, there was a sudden flash of light and to the horror of the people present Sir Robert's ghost appeared and offered to cease haunting the area if they would stop the exorcism.

What happened then is not clear, but the haunting continued – and in Buckinghamshire's tales of the supernatural, wicked Bobby Banistre has never been forgotten.

Another ghost whose story has persisted over the centuries is the Green Man of Fingest, a character whose reputation in life was every bit as reprehensible as Bobby Banistre's.

Henry Burghersh became Bishop of Lincoln in 1320. At the age of 28, he was young to be a bishop but having failed in his ambition to become Bishop of Winchester, Henry managed to bribe his way into the Bishopric of Lincoln. In those days Fingest was administered by the Bishops of Lincoln, who had a palace there 'half a furlong above the church', in the grounds of the present Fingest Manor House. The 18th-century Browne-Willis manuscripts mention that 'several foundations and pavements were dug up which showed it to be of large extent.'

Henry was granted 'Free Warren', or sporting

rights, in his manor of Fingest, and he enjoyed hunting through the surrounding countryside and woodland. He owned Hanger Wood and Mill Hanging Wood but this was not enough for him. He was granted a licence 'to impark three hundred acres of land enjoining' the land he already owned, which was bad news for the village people, as it meant that the common land they had always used was now lost to them.

The commoners were left with around 100 acres, which was totally inadequate for their needs, and they suffered great poverty and distress. Naturally, the people of Fingest felt great hatred for the rapacious bishop. And in their hatred they cursed the soul of Henry Burghersh, and with all their hearts they wished doom on the selfish, black-hearted churchman who had caused them so much hardship.

Henry died in 1340, and retribution followed swiftly. Not long after his death, a forester dressed in green, with a bow, quiver and horn, appeared in Fingest churchyard to a friend of Burghersh, who was astonished to recognise the former bishop. The dejected and miserable spectre bewailed his fate, explaining that, because he had seized the common land to make his park, he was condemned for eternity to roam the woods and land he had stolen in the guise of a forester. He begged that the land should be restored to the people, but perhaps this was not enough to save Henry's soul, as Fingest's Green Man continued to haunt the area for long afterwards.

Ghosts
at the Chequers

'THE pub was exorcised about 13 years ago, but people still say there are ghosts here' mused Jim Ryan, the landlord. 'An Australian lady was sitting in the corner two or three years ago. She was interested in the paranormal and said "You have ghosts here, haven't you? I tried to get up three times, and every time I was pressed back down by your ghost."'

He smiled, 'I try to rationalise everything I see – even when sometimes I notice a fleeting shadow.'

The ancient Chequers Inn on the fringe of Amersham is a delightful place, with gleaming horse brasses, open fireplaces and low mind-your-head beams. It is cosy and welcoming, and yet there are dark memories in its history, linked to the days when people were burnt at the stake for their religious beliefs.

On a hill above St Mary's church in Market Square, Amersham you will find the Martyrs' Memorial. The inscription reads 'The Noble Army of Martyrs Praise Thee – Amersham Martyrs. They died for the principles of religious liberty, for the right to read and interpret the Holy Scriptures and to worship God according to their consciences as revealed through God's Holy Word.' Here, in 1506 and 1521, members of the Lollard movement were burnt to death after refusing to recant their beliefs, their own children having been forced to light the faggots on each occasion.

Tradition says that a group of religious dissenters, six men and a woman, spent the night at the Chequers under the guard of a warder, before they met their cruel death the following day. This may refer to a previous building on the same site, as the inn you see today is said to date back to the late 17th century.

A succession of families have experienced supernatural disturbances at the Chequers and, although the building has been exorcised on several occasions, as the present landlord relates, 'people still say there are ghosts here'.

An exorcism had been performed in 1953 but when a former private detective became the licensee there in 1963, it was only a few weeks after moving in that he heard screams coming from his daughters' bedroom one night.

He found eight year old Julie and her eleven year old sister, Maralyn, clinging together, shaking with fear. Julie told him through her tears that she had seen a white, hooded figure drift into the bedroom. It had passed round the dressing table and disappeared out of the door. The bedroom door was usually kept closed to prevent the dog getting in, but the girls' father had found it open when he arrived.

The landlord made a thorough search, afraid that an intruder might have broken in, but when he found nothing he felt even more alarmed at the thought that the little girl might really have seen something supernatural. And, after that, the whole family were disturbed and frightened, night after night, by eerie moaning and screaming noises that defied explanation. Doors would open of their own accord, the atmosphere became icy cold at times, and the dog, a large alsatian, was obviously scared by something. It was unnerving, and after a cleaner who slept in the attic insisted that she had seen a ghost, the landlord's wife was too frightened to stay in the inn on her own.

At such times there are always sceptics ready with rational explanations for the most bizarre happenings, and a reporter from the local paper, accompanied by an Amersham resident, spent the night in the Chequers in an attempt to sort the pub's troublesome spirit out once and for all. They decided that the eerie screaming was simply caused by a passing owl, strange cold spots were just draughts and the appearance of a ghostly figure was nothing but a trick of the light reflected in a mirror. And, in an old building like the Chequers, the contraction and expansion of beams could cause doors to open of their own volition.

Unconvinced, the family decided to enlist the services of a medium. She was able to get in touch with the ghost, and said he had told her that he was a local man called Auden who had been obliged to act as goaler to the group of religious dissenters held prisoner at the inn the night before they were due to be burnt at the stake. It was due to his troubled conscience that his distressed spirit was now earthbound.

For a time after the medium's visit there was an improvement, but in 1964 a clergyman had to be called upon to perform another service of exorcism. This seems to have had a beneficial effect until 1971, when a Scottish barman told the landlady, Mrs Vera Hill, that he had seen the apparition of a man in a long dark cloak 'trying to get up the chimney'.

Mrs Hill had noticed nothing herself but,

nevertheless, she had no doubt that her pub was haunted. 'We discussed the apparition with some locals immediately afterwards', she said, 'and they assured us that it was Mr Osman who had been seen many times over the last few years.'

It seems likely that 'Osman' and 'Auden' were one and the same.

On another occasion, the ghost of a woman with a kind, lovely face, and wearing a long robe, appeared in the bar – and then vanished. Was she the woman who was one of the martyrs? And, after nearly 400 years, does their conscience-stricken goaler still linger in the place where they spent the last troubled night before their awful ordeal? Time will tell.

Echoes of the Past at Chenies

HENRY VIII paid many visits to Chenies Manor in his lifetime, and ghostly echoes of the past can still be heard in this delightful old house which has known many of history's VIPs. The first Earl of Bedford entertained Henry and Anne Boleyn, and their baby daughter Elizabeth, there in 1534, but when Henry came again in 1542, poor Anne was no more, and Henry brought another ill-fated beauty, his fifth wife, Catherine Howard.

For the young and lively Catherine, seven years younger than Henry's daughter Mary, her ageing husband with his painful, ulcerated leg must have been a depressing prospect. She had spent a light-hearted and promiscuous girlhood in the household of her grandmother, the Duchess of Norfolk, and although she was Anne Boleyn's cousin, regardless of Anne's dire fate, Catherine recklessly began an affair with the dashing Thomas Culpeper. Culpeper was one of the King's attendants who accompanied them to Chenies, and the two lovers took the opportunity to pursue their passionate liaison. As we know, their relationship would later lead to death on the scaffold for them both, and Catherine would become one of the most famous phantoms of Hampton Court, where her ghost has often been heard running down the Long Gallery, screaming for Henry's forgiveness.

For many years the heavy footsteps of a limping man have been heard on the stairs at Chenies, and in the gallery approaching the bedroom where Catherine probably slept. Was it Henry keeping a suspicious eye on his unfaithful wife or simply paying a nocturnal visit to his rose without a thorn in the days before he was persuaded of her frailty? It is curious that after all these centuries Henry still has a gammy leg. And yet it seems that this is how his ghost is identified, as groans and slow, dragging footsteps heard in the cloisters at Windsor Castle are also assumed to be Henry, who used to take a little painful exercise there when his leg prevented anything more strenuous.

Chenies Manor has a remarkable set of ornamental chimneys, said to be the best of their period, and there is no doubt that Henry admired them. He was enlarging Hampton Court at that time and the workmen responsible for the rebuilding of Chenies Manor were engaged to produce chimneys just as splendid for Hampton Court.

Queen Elizabeth was another frequent visitor to Chenies, entertained by Francis, the second Earl of Bedford, as her father, Henry, had been by Francis's father, John Russell, the first Earl, whose wife inherited Chenies from the Cheyne family.

At the time of the Civil War, the fourth Earl was a friend of John Hampden, who famously refused to pay Ship Money, Charles I's tax to support the navy. It was not Hampden's first act of defiance questioning Charles' absolute monarchy and, when the Civil War began, Hampden was a strong Parliamentary supporter. His splendid statue in Cromwellian armour stands in Aylesbury town centre.

A detachment of Cromwell's Roundheads were

quartered at Chenies in the armoury, which is a long gallery stretching for 144 ft. Lt Col Alastair MacLeod Matthews, the present occupant of Chenies with his wife Elizabeth, told me that their staff say they sometimes hear thudding and tinkling laughter in the armoury, which is situated above their quarters. 'Civil War soldiers larking about with the village girls?' he wonders.

He also related that from a memo written early in the last century it appears that a headless man then walked in the ornamental ground south of the house. This was thought to be the ghost of Lord William Russell, who was beheaded in Lincolns Inn Fields around 1670, where there is a plaque commemorating the event, and whose body was returned for burial at Chenies. 'Doors then often opened by themselves, and they sometimes seem to still', Colonel Matthews told me.

Chenies Manor is a delightful and interesting place, and the gardens around the house attract many visitors, especially in the spring, to see the glorious display of thousands of tulips. There are many relics of the past, such as a 13th-century stone crypt, a medieval well and a Tudor privy in a closet which opens off the library. The history of Chenies is full of entertaining sidelights, such as Edward I's visit when he arrived with a camel! The record of this momentous occasion also notes that it was Easter, and 130 eggs were hard boiled and presented to the people of the village, said to be the first known reference to Easter eggs.

Small wonder that a house which has been in the path of history for centuries should be so full of memories that sometimes they are almost tangible. From the time that Colonel Matthews and his wife moved into Chenies Manor in the 1950s, they noticed ghostly footsteps and creaking floorboards in the night, as well as the doors that opened of their own accord.

'But I must say that none of this worries us,' says the Colonel, 'We always feel that we live in a very happy house.'

5

Murder at Ye Old Ostrich Inn

THE splendid half-timbered Ostrich Inn at Colnbrook, with its flags flying, claims to be Britain's third oldest hostelry, and although the present building dates from about 1400, it has a history going back to 1106. At that time the 'hospice of Colebroc' was given to the abbey at Abingdon to be held in trust 'for the good of travellers in this world, and the salvation of their souls in the next'. In the light of these words, it is sad to think what happened to some of them.

Inside the inn is a fine example of a picturesque, oak-beamed, traditional English pub, with coach lamps, copper pans, horse brasses and pewter tankards on the walls, and dried hops festooning the bar. Over one fireplace is a collection of old guns and swords, and in solitary splendour on another wall is a large businesslike weapon. This is Dick Turpin's pistol, or so it is believed. The story goes that the famous highwayman had a narrow escape from the Bow Street Runners one day while he was relaxing at the Ostrich. He jumped from his bedroom window into the courtyard, mounted his waiting horse, and got clean away, but presumably left his pistol behind.

The inn stands on Colnbrook's narrow High Street, and today planes arriving at Heathrow skim the tops of the trees nearby. This was the Old Bath Road, a busy route for travellers, and many rich and important people called at the Ostrich on their way to Windsor.

There is a tradition that King John paused there on his way to sign Magna Carta at Runnymede, and on the map one can trace where an old road used to be that would have been a direct route there.

Centuries ago the area between Colnbrook and Longford became notorious for vagabonds and highwaymen, and the landlord of the Ostrich in those days had his own particular interest in wealthy merchants who sought his hospitality.

A book called *Thomas of Reading* by Thomas Deloney, published in 1632, tells the macabre story of mine host, the murderous Jarman, and his equally rapacious wife, and the awful fate that befell unwary travellers who went to sleep in the inn's Blue Room, never to wake again...

This room was immediately above the kitchen and had a trapdoor in the floor. By the removal of a couple of bolts, the bed would tip the sleeping occupant through the trapdoor and into a waiting vat of boiling water in the kitchen below. According to Deloney, 'In the dead time of night, when the victim was sound asleep, they plucked out the bolts, and down would the man fall out of his bed into the boiling cauldron, and all the cloaths that were upon him, where being suddenly scalded and drowned, he was never able to cry or speak one word.'

The Jarmans would then remove the man's belongings from the room, together with his money and valuables, and hide his horse. 'And then,' said Deloney, 'lifting up the said falling floor which hung by the hinges, they made it fast as before. The dead body they would take presently out of the cauldron and throw it down the river, which ran near unto their house, whereby they escaped all danger.'

A man called Thomas Cole often stayed at the Ostrich, and he and his little grey donkey were well known in Colnbrook. The evil Jarmans had him in mind as a future victim, but fate seemed determined to foil their plans. Once he was ill and stopped off at another inn, and once he went to see a fire in London, and on yet another occasion a friend was with him.

But the time came when it looked as if Thomas Cole had at last fallen into their hands. He seemed in low spirits that night, almost as if he had some premonition of what was about to happen. In fact, he decided to make his will and asked Jarman if he would witness it. Blackhearted as he was, this upset Jarman and he suggested to his wife that they should reconsider their evil plan. But she would have none of this weakness, and when Cole was sleeping soundly after the quart of burnt sack they had given him, they withdrew the bolts and he was pitched into the cauldron below, as so many others had been before him.

But there were to be no more occupants of the deadly bed at the Ostrich inn. Thomas Cole's donkey got loose and was found wandering on the highway by some people who knew his owner. They caught the animal and went back to the inn with him, and when Jarman saw them coming, he panicked and ran off.

This behaviour aroused suspicion and the justices were told, and when Jarman's wife was arrested, she confessed everything. Jarman had got as far as Windsor Forest before the law caught up with him, but catch up with him it did, and the evil pair were tried and executed, declaring at the end that Mr Cole had been their 60th victim.

In the bar of the Ostrich Inn today you can see a model of the four poster bed, above the kitchen with the waiting cauldron below, and, by turning a little key, you can see how the bed tips and the trapdoor opens, pitching the unfortunate occupant to his death. There is also a photograph of an earlier four poster made of mahogany, its details taken from Thomas Deloney's book.

The river is quite near the back of the inn, and today is fast flowing, and one can quite easily imagine the midnight scene as Jarman and his wife carried some unlucky traveller's body to be borne away by the water. But did they really dispose of 60 victims? Did no one wonder how it was so many well-to-do travellers managed to get drowned? And did no inquisitive servant or visitor happen to notice that there was something unusual about the Blue Room? I wonder, too, if Sweeney Todd ever happened to come across Thomas Deloney's book. He would have found it quite inspiring.

One would expect the Ostrich Inn to have supernatural echoes of its gruesome history, and it is said that the ghost of Thomas Cole, the Jarman's last victim, has haunted the inn for centuries, but apparently, according to staff, he has not put in an appearance recently.

6

The Cavalier
of Claydon House

HE has sad eyes, this old cavalier who, after 350 years, still patrols his former home. Van Dyck's portrait of Edmund Verney, which hangs in the Saloon at Claydon House, has captured the sensitive, troubled face of a man who never failed his King, even when his heart was not in it.

Edmund Verney looks down from the wall of a house much changed from the one he knew when he and his family moved into the old manor in 1620. The Verneys had owned land in Middle Claydon since the 15th century, but it had been leased to the Gifford family, who built the house, and when the lease ran out, Edmund borrowed the money to redeem it.

Although the son of a prosperous father, Edmund was always hard-up for, by the time the estate passed to him, his elder brother Francis had dissipated his inheritance and sold off family properties during the course of an adventurous life. A colourful character, Francis fought for the Turks in the Holy Land, then turned Barbary pirate, was captured and spent years as a galley slave, finally dying in hospital at Messina.

Edmund was devoted to his wife Margaret and twelve children, although his duties at Court often kept him away from home. He had entered the service of Prince Henry, James I's eldest son, in 1611, when he came of age, but the Prince died soon afterwards and Edmund joined the household of Prince Charles.

When Charles became King, he made Edmund Knight Marshal of the Palace, and attendance at Court was a further drain on his resources. Charles was also permanently short of money, and often borrowed from Edmund, notably £1,000 'for supply of our most urgent affairs', money which was never fully repaid.

The Verneys were great letter writers and when Sir Harry Verney married Parthenope Nightingale in 1858, they found at the top of the house a wainscoted gallery 40 ft long, full of boxes on trestles, containing bundles of letters and papers, account books, rent rolls, recipes and love letters, a treasure trove dating from before 1460 up to 1810.

Parthenope undertook the colossal task of editing these letters and *The Memoirs of the Verney Family* gives a unique picture of their lives, loves, family doings and everyday problems in what were often dangerous and troubled times, bringing them as vividly alive to the reader as people of our own time. Some of the letters are exhibited in cases upstairs at Claydon House.

The Civil War divided many families, including the Verneys. Sir Edmund's sympathies were with the Parliamentary cause, which was supported by Ralph, his eldest son, but he felt he must remain loyal to the King.

'I have eaten his bread,' he wrote, 'served him for nearly thirty years, and I will not do so base a thing as to forsake him, but choose rather to lose my life (which I am sure I shall do) to preserve and defend those things which are against my conscience to preserve and defend.'

Charles made Edmund Verney his Standard Bearer, and at the battle of Edgehill in 1642 the old knight courageously 'adventured with the standard in order that the soldiers might be engaged to follow him'. He was surrounded by hundreds of pikemen and musketeers when the battle started on the afternoon of October 23rd, and in the fierce fighting Sir Edmund was seen using his heavy standard as a pike until the top broke off. He saw his own valet, Jason, killed and Sir Edward Sydenham, fighting nearby, reported afterwards that Sir Edmund 'killed two with his owne hands, whereof one had killed Jason, and broke the point of his standard at push of pike before he fell.'

He is said to have been offered his life by a throng of enemies on condition that he would surrender the standard, but his reply was that his life was his own, but the standard was his and their sovereign's, and he would not deliver it while he lived.

Although he was struck down and killed, Sir Edmund firmly gripped the standard even in death, and his hand was hacked off to capture it. After the battle the lanes and fields were strewn with the bodies of the dead, and more than 4,000 were buried, many where they lay.

Sir Edmund's body was never found, but his hand, identified by the ring that King Charles had given him, was returned to the family. The ring has a miniature of the King and is, of course, a cherished family heirloom.

The story of the ghostly re-enactment of the battle of Edgehill is well known. On 23rd January 1643 a pamphlet was published which described how during the night of the Saturday before Christmas some shepherds saw an amazing sight. There appeared in the air in front of them a phantom battle of Edgehill, being re-fought with all its dreadful sights and sounds just as it had been in reality. They stood petrified, afraid to move, watching for around three hours before it all vanished.

The following night it all happened again, and again a week later. King Charles heard about it and sent some officers to investigate and they, too, witnessed the same phenomenon, recognising in the apparitions some of their dead friends, including Sir Edmund.

This was only the beginning of Sir Edmund's ghostly appearances. For centuries his disconsolate ghost was said to haunt Claydon House and grounds, often seen peering sadly through the windows.

In a book called *The Standard Bearer* by Peter Verney, published in 1963, he writes, 'Sir Edmund is an active ghost, for he is still said to haunt Claydon where he performs a ceaseless vigil for his lost hand. He is reputed to come only in times of trouble, doubtless to see if he can help in any way, so it seems his "kindness and courtesy to the poorest" lingers even in death.'

Some years ago when the large ballroom was demolished, the estate carpenter working there looked up to see a man, wearing strange old-fashioned clothes, standing nearby unhappily eyeing the devastation. He did not recognise the person, and called out to him, whereupon which the figure vanished.

Miss Ruth Verney had an interesting encounter with what seems to have been Sir Edmund's ghost when she was a young girl in about 1892. She described running up the Red Stairs and turning left, and left again on the first landing, walking towards the Cedar Room. She noticed a man halfway down from the upper floor, but had continued on her way before it suddenly occurred to her to wonder who he could be. She ran back to look, but the man had gone. He had been on the third step of the second flight coming down, and she felt sure there hadn't been time for him to get to the top or the bottom of the stairs from where she had seen him.

Ruth described him as tall and slender, wearing a long black cloak, beneath the hem of which she could see the tip of a sword. He was carrying a black hat with a white feather gracefully curled round the crown.

There are various stories of unexplained footsteps being heard along a passage known as the haunted corridor in the oldest part of the house. When I visited Claydon House, now a National Trust property, at the end of the 1994 season, I was told by a member of staff that Sir Edmund was seen during the last war riding his horse in the grounds, and also in the old part of the house.

Major Sir Ralph Verney was quoted in the *Bucks Advertiser* on the 6th March 1975, when he said 'I cannot claim to have seen his ghost myself, but my Mother and sisters have. He seems to appear more often on special occasions, and at the Coronation of George VI in 1937 when great parties were held here at Claydon, he was seen a great deal.

'During the war when we had a girls' school here, the Head Mistress who seemed to be slightly psychic, kept on meeting him.'

Some of the staff occupy apartments in the top of the house and I was told that recently they had been conscious of a strange atmosphere, and footsteps had been heard several times walking along the corridor outside – 'but no one liked to look out!'

When Parthenope Verney lived at Claydon her sister Florence Nightingale was a frequent visitor in her later years. Florence's bedroom and sitting room can be seen and in the museum are interesting photographs and memorabilia. It's said that her lectures on hygiene to village women were not always well received, but her help in founding one of the county's first free libraries at Steeple Claydon was much appreciated.

We are told that Florence Nightingale was very attached to Claydon, and she left a tangible memorial in the cedar and cypress trees near the house, which were grown from seeds she brought back from the Crimea. One night when Andrew Lang, the author, was sleeping in the Rose Room, which is near Miss Nightingale's bedroom, he woke and saw a mysterious 'grey lady'. She disappeared into the wall where a secret room was once discovered when the building was being repaired. Could it have been the Lady with the Lamp herself adding her presence to that of the gallant and benevolent Sir Edmund, in this much-loved family home?

7

Gentlemen (and Ladies) of the Road

WHEN it comes to the Ghost with the Most – haunts that is – one must admit that Anne Boleyn has the edge. But Dick Turpin runs her a close second. Throughout the country there are many inns which claim to have been one of his hideaways and the spectral figure of the famous highwayman is still said to ride at times along lanes and ancient tracks where once he plied his nefarious trade.

Buckinghamshire knew Turpin well, and Watling Street was one of his stamping grounds, where many an unlucky traveller had reason to rue an encounter with this ruthless gentleman of the road.

His ghost has been seen on an ancient way called Bury Lane, near Woughton, possibly making for the Old Swan Inn at Woughton on the Green, which was one of his regular ports of call. Tradition says that it was here he reversed his horse's shoes and fooled his pursuers into going the wrong way while he escaped to safety. The landlord at the Old Swan in those days is believed to have had a sympathetic attitude to miscreants such as Turpin, and many a ruffian who reached the old inn ahead of the hue and cry was sure of a safe hideout until the danger was passed.

Someone else who gave Turpin protection, but through fear rather than favour, was the owner of an old manor house in Weathercock Lane, Aspley Guise, just over the Bedfordshire border. Turpin took cover in the wine cellar of the house on one occasion and while there made a gruesome find. In a cupboard he came upon the bodies of the young daughter of the house and her lover, shot by her father who had chanced upon their secret assignation when he went down to the cellar for his whisky nightcap. Naturally, this was the kind of power Turpin knew how to use, and as the price of his silence he blackmailed the house's owner into letting him use the cellar as a hideout whenever he wanted.

Turpin met his end long ago, but his ghost still returns from time to time to Weathercock Lane. An eye witness once reported hearing the sound of horse's hooves, and to his amazement the famous highwayman passed by him into the courtyard and faded into the wall of the building. He commented, 'It was not an alarming experience, except that Turpin looks a much tougher character than popular fancy supposes.'

Someone who saw an unidentified highwayman was Mr Dave Robson, who was walking home from the Bull Hotel, Gerrards Cross, where he worked. The *Bucks Free Press* reported on 10th February 1984 that it was about midnight when Mr Robson first noticed the sound of horse's hooves. 'Through the haze I could clearly pick out a man with a gun dressed in a big cloak and a black hat,' he said. 'He rode past me and disappeared by a group of trees.'

Was it another sighting of Turpin, or one of his fellow gentlemen of the road, still lying in wait for one of the spectral coaches that, despite ever increasing traffic on most roads, are still occasionally seen, following their former routes, to the amazement of any witness?

For instance, there have been many tales of unseen coaches heard passing along the Oxford Road, Beaconsfield. During the 1920s, the sounds of a coach's wheels were heard night after night, approaching Beaconsfield from the direction of Gerrards Cross, but although the sounds appeared to continue along the road, nothing was ever seen.

It was well over 100 years ago that a coach left Beaconsfield one foggy night, after stopping to change horses. At the bottom of the hill leading to Wycombe End, Beaconsfield, the horses mistook their direction in the fog and ended up in a deep pond. It was a tragedy as everyone involved lost their lives, and for years, on the anniversary, the cries of the dying could be heard in the vicinity, calling for help.

A ghostly coach and horses have sometimes been seen waiting outside the Greyhound pub in Chalfont St Peter, while another equipage has been spotted thundering through Finnamore Wood, near Marlow, and yet another on the road from Radnage Bottom to Bennetts End.

In the 18th century, an unfortunate farmhand called Clark was killed when he fell from his horse, and for many years afterwards it was believed to be his restless spirit which brought terror to anyone who happened to be in the area of Hogback Wood, Forty Green and Penn during the night.

The ghost was particularly troublesome in 1880, when four farmers, fortified perhaps by some strong ale, decided to do a spot of ghost-busting. They were not disappointed. As they rode along, the phantom rider appeared suddenly through a hedge and galloped off ahead of them. The eerie thing was that his horse's hooves made no sound. They set off in pursuit, and when they reached Penn church, the apparition turned and laughed at them, disappearing in a 'grey mist'. This was too much for the farmers' own horses, which bolted in fright.

Next day the farmers went back to where they had seen the mysterious rider disappear, but they found only the hoof prints of four horses, not five!

A delightful ghost known as the Spangled Lady has been seen to appear from Sandage Wood, High Wycombe. With her jewelry sparkling prettily in the moonlight, she walks to a gate where she stands looking out before retracing her steps into the wood. Is she waiting for a lover who never comes? For how many disappointing years has she been all dressed up in her best with no one to appreciate her charms? One cannot help thinking that Dick Turpin would be happy to meet her.

The Lady in Red is another ghost which inspires sympathy. She is said to have been Anna, a young girl of Lane End who planned to marry her sweetheart in 1766. But only ten days before the wedding, Anna fell ill and died.

A few years later, a ghost was seen wandering on country paths in the Park Lane area near the pub at Wheelerend Common where Anna used to work. In life she had been so fond of the colour red that she had always worn it, and therefore when an apparition dressed in red was seen, everyone assumed it was Anna's ghost. Her appearances were quite frequent in the mid-19th century.

Then, in 1943, a girl walking across a field towards Hanover Hill saw someone in a red dress. It was a cold December day, and snowing, and the lady in red had no coat. Was it Anna? Her appearances were quite commonplace in the 1940s, and she was seen again in the 1960s, usually in the afternoon.

A ghostly woman rider often seen galloping fast down Loakes Lane, High Wycombe is believed to have been thrown by her horse in the 17th century.

To the west of Great Missenden a more alarming equestrienne rides at a furious speed over the hills between Stoney Green and Bryant's Bottom, holding her head in her hand.

Ghostlore teems with tales of headless horses and riders, even coaches drawn by headless steeds and driven by headless coachmen. It all sounds like a macabre bit of ancient folklore meant to chill the blood of the gullible as they sit round the fire on dark stormy nights. Who, you may ask, has seen either a headless horse or a headless rider lately?

Well, as a matter of fact, while I was writing this book I was told about the experience of five teenage girls who will not easily forget what happened to them as recently as 1995.

The five friends decided to go camping and they chose to pitch their tents in a field beside a wood at West Wycombe. It was a lot of fun, and there was so much talk and laughter that 1 am found them still awake. Then something happened. They became aware of a weird noise that was hard to identify. It was something like the howling noise the wind makes on a stormy night, or perhaps, they thought, it could be some animal. Whatever it was, the girls didn't like it. In the dark, that strange howling sound was terrifying.

After a few minutes the noise stopped, but suddenly there was a bright flashing light which illuminated the tents. Fearfully two of the girls lifted their tent flap and looked outside, but there was nothing to see, and the light had gone as suddenly as it had appeared.

Then the howling began again. It was very loud,

and with one accord the girls got up and went outside. This time there was something to see. To their amazement a huge white horse was galloping across the field, but it was about a metre above ground level, and they were horrified to see that its rider was headless!

The girls say it was the most terrifying thing that had ever happened to them – and when five people are absolutely certain that they have seen the same thing, chances are they really did!

Cavaliers and Roundheads have been spotted in the lanes around Wycombe, and they say John Hampden himself comes riding across the fields with his Greencoats on moonlight nights.

A terrifying horseman used to tear through Great Missenden at dead of night, and it seems probable that this story may relate to eccentric Captain Backhouse. He was a 19th-century soldier, whose will instructed that when he died he should be buried in the back garden of his house at Havenfields, standing upright, his battle sword in his hand!

Despite his rather unusual wishes having been followed, villagers were convinced that it was Captain Backhouse's ghost which continued to ride through the village at night, waving his sword in a horrifying manner, and permission was sought to re-inter his body in Great Missenden churchyard. This was done, and there were no more midnight rides to disturb the village.

Ghostly jaywalkers, with an alarming habit of rushing out in front of passing cars, are a hazard in some parts of the country. The shocked motorist, under the impression that he has hit a pedestrian, draws up and gets out to see what has happened. Invariably there is no body, the car is undamaged, and the shaken driver goes on, at a loss to understand his unnerving experience.

Two motor cyclists had similar encounters at Pednor Bottom, near Chesham. As the first one rode along he noticed a figure dressed in black, sitting on a gate, and as he got nearer, the figure suddenly jumped from the gate right in front of him. 'I didn't stand a chance,' he said afterwards, 'I hit him full on. But when I stopped and looked, there was no one there. I've never got away from a place so fast.'

The second cyclist was riding along the same stretch of road a week later, and exactly the same thing happened.

As Alison Uttley said in her book on Buckinghamshire, there are haunted woods and lanes where uncanny things have happened and might occur again. One old countryman knowingly remarked of such a place, 'That's a road I would not like to go along at night. It's terrible lonely, and you aren't alone, either.'

Who hasn't experienced that chilling feeling in some quiet, remote place that unseen eyes are watching, and that you are not welcome there... It is then that you unwillingly recall stories of frightening phantoms, of headless horses, and huge black hounds with eyes like carriage lamps padding silently along in the darkness. Or perhaps you wonder if there could still be such things as fairies and goblins.

Alison Uttley recalls the experience of a friend who witnessed a group of the little people in a garden near the Icknield Way. They were about two ft high, golden yellow, dancing lightheartedly in a ring. They were so beautiful, the watcher was filled with happiness to have seen such a rare and enchanting sight, but just as suddenly as they had appeared, they were gone.

It seems that there are still strange, unlikely things to be seen for those who have eyes to see them. And in Buckinghamshire too!

8

The Poisoner's Tale

NO calendar of Buckinghamshire would be complete without a picture of the white-timbered watermill at Hambleden, mirrored in the river Thames. Alison Uttley called it the most beautiful place in the Thames Valley, and indeed the whole area of the Hambleden Valley includes some of the most delightful villages in the Chilterns, Turville, Fingest, Skirmett and Frieth.

One of the Turville's claims to fame, apart from its picturesque charm, is a 19th-century Rip Van Winkle remembered as the Sleeping Girl of Turville, who slumbered for a period variously described as seven or nine years. She lived in a cottage near the church known as Sleepy House, and was a constant source of interest to people who came from far and wide to see her. Her devoted mother kept her nourished, using a teapot to feed her with port wine and sugar. Apparently her mother died after a fall downstairs and not long afterwards her daughter awoke from her long nap, got married and had children. One wonders if her extended sleep could possibly have been nothing more than a drunken stupor due to too much port?

The Hambleden Valley area claims another famous character as a local ghost. Mary Blandy, the 18th-century woman hung for poisoning her father, used to visit Turville Court, and Churchfield Wood must have been a favourite spot for a ride, as her ghost on a white horse has been seen there. One can imagine that she may have found solace in her lifetime in this beautiful place as she pondered her problems with the unreliable Captain Cranstoun and his 'love philtres' that were to lead her to the scaffold.

Mary Blandy seems to be an active ghost, as local people say she has often been seen walking down the lane that leads to Dolsden Farm, which would have been a bridlepath in her day. Elizabeth Wiltshire, who has made an interesting collection of ghost stories of the valley, tells of her grandfather's encounter with Mary Blandy's ghost one clear moonlight night.

The lane up from Dolsden Farm is steep and Wilfred Wiltshire was pushing his bicycle along there when he noticed someone approaching. In the bright moonlight he could see that it was a woman in strangely old-fashioned clothes and, as she got nearer, he could hear the rustle of her skirts. Because it was late for a woman to be out alone, he thought that she might be frightened at meeting a man in that lonely lane and he did not acknowledge her presence as they drew level. Then, deciding it might have been more reassuring if he had raised his cap and said 'Goodnight', he turned, but to his alarm, although he could still hear the rustle of her skirt, the figure had vanished! He hurried home, white and shaken, and told his wife 'I've just seen a ghost.'

Other people have had a similar uncanny experience in the same area. In *The Buckinghamshire Dialect*, H. Harman recounts another first-hand report by a Turville resident. 'One dark night my wife and I were walking down the road . . . we saw something pass us and heard the rustling of a silk dress. My wife nearly fainted . . . I turned to see what it was, but could see nothing. It really upset my wife, and she has never forgotten it.'

Mary Blandy lived just over the border in Henley, where her father was a solicitor and the Town Clerk. Francis Blandy was a busy and prosperous man, ambitious that his only child, Mary, born in 1720, should make a happy and successful marriage. With this in mind he made no attempt to discount rumours that Mary's future inheritance would be in the region of £30,000. So Mary was considered quite a 'catch', although she was no beauty. In fact, although she had a good figure and striking black eyes, her face was described as 'rather ordinary, not improved by the results of small-pox'.

Francis Blandy intended that Mary's future husband should be something better than the local talent provided, and he and his wife took Mary to Bath, as many parents with marriageable daughters did in those days.

There Mary proved to be quite a success, and there were several candidates for her hand. As we know from Jane Austen's descriptions of the social scene at Bath, there was nothing like a gallant soldier to set female hearts a-flutter, and Mary formed an attachment to one of her beaux, a captain, who was unfortunately ordered abroad with his regiment almost immediately.

However, this was a love match never destined to reach fulfilment, as fate in the shape of one Captain William Henry Cranstoun was waiting in the wings.

In the summer of 1746, Mary and her parents were invited to dinner at Paradise House, the home of General Mark Kerr. Captain Cranstoun, in Henley on a recruiting mission, was staying with the General and he and Mary were mutually attracted. Cranstoun must have had a charm of manner which did not rely on his physical appearance, as he is described as being short and ordinary looking, with sandy hair, small, weak eyes, a freckled and pitted skin, and 'clumsy legs'. He was known to have a roving eye, but to Mr and Mrs Blandy he was highly eligible due to the fact that he was the fifth son of a Scots peer, Lord Cranstoun.

During the summer of 1747, when Cranstoun again visited Henley, he declared his love for Mary. Although he made a casual reference to a Scottish lady who he said was falsely claiming to be his wife, Mary accepted his proposal. Her parents welcomed him with open arms and he came to stay with them for a time.

But Nemesis in the shape of a letter from a relative of Cranstoun's soon followed. It informed Mr Blandy that Cranstoun already had a wife and child in Scotland, having married Anne Murray in 1744. As she was a Jacobite and a Roman Catholic, the alliance had been kept secret lest it damaged his chances of promotion.

Mr Blandy was furious, but Mary and her mother believed Cranstoun's protestations that there would soon be an annulment. Attempts to get the marriage contract put aside failed, however, and the court declared Cranstoun legally married. He was, moreover, ordered to pay his wife an annuity, an unwelcome outcome he kept to himself.

Mrs Blandy's health deteriorated, and in September 1749 she died. Cranstoun had lost an ally and Mr Blandy now became increasingly unfriendly towards Cranstoun, and made no secret of the fact that his visits to the house were unwelcome.

Cranstoun told Mary about a wise woman he knew

in Scotland whose 'love powders' acted like magic, and promised that if she gave some to her father they would make him more amenable to their relationship. Mary had her doubts, but later she recalled that one day, when her father was in a particularly angry mood, Cranstoun put some of his magic powder into Mr Blandy's tea and the old man became much more cheerful. This convinced her that her plausible lover could be right after all.

Cranstoun returned to Scotland early in 1751, from where he sent Mary some of the 'love philtres' to give to her father, with the result that Mr Blandy became very ill with pain and sickness. Their maid, Susan, happened to taste a cup of tea intended for Mr Blandy and was ill for a week afterwards. And, on another occasion, the family's old charwoman drank some of his tea, with similar results.

On the 5th August 1751, Mary gave her father some gruel for his supper and he became so ill in the night that they had to call the apothecary. Next day, poor Mr Blandy was given more gruel, with the same results. And, later, when the cook brought the remains of his supper downstairs, the charwoman ate it and became violently sick.

When Mary wanted to give her father more of the same gruel, the maid protested that it was now too stale. She and the cook were becoming suspicious, and when they examined the gruel pan, they discovered some white, gritty substance at the bottom. They hid the pan in a locked cupboard overnight.

Mary's uncle, the Reverend Stevens, arrived on the 9th August, and Susan told him about their suspicions. Next day they told Mr Blandy they thought he was being poisoned. Even so, the old man trustingly drank the tea Mary gave him at breakfast, simply complaining that it had a gritty taste.

In the light of these events, it is hard to believe that Mary did not know the true nature of Cranstoun's powders. The fact that Susan and the cook were eyeing her with suspicion was not lost on her, and she took Cranstoun's letters and what was left of the powder and threw them on the kitchen fire. With great presence of mind, the cook immediately put some more coal on the fire and, when Mary had gone, was able to rescue the paper packet still containing some of the white substance.

Meanwhile, Mr Blandy was deteriorating fast and the doctor had no doubt that his patient had been poisoned. When he left, he took with him the sediment from the gruel pan and the packet the cook had rescued from the fire.

Mr Blandy died on the 14th August 1741, forgiving his daughter and warning her yet again about the treacherous Cranstoun. Too late, Mary Blandy realised what she had done and, full of remorse, she ran from the house, down Hart Street and over the bridge to the Angel Inn. But angry Henley residents followed her there, and she was taken to Oxford where she was tried for murder on the 29th February 1752.

She was found guilty and hung on 6th April 1752, protesting her innocence to the end. After her death, Mary's body was brought back to Henley and buried at night between the graves of her parents in the presence of an enormous crowd of local people. Was it just curiosity that brought them there, or did they see her not as a murderer but rather as an innocent girl used by a heartless villain?

Cranstoun himself did not live long after her. On

the 2nd December the same year he died at Furnes, near Dunkirk, of a strange illness which caused him to swell enormously and to expire in great agony. He was 46 years old.

With such a history, Mary Blandy's return to her former haunts as a ghost seems not unexpected, and over the years any unexplained apparition within range of Henley was automatically claimed to be the notorious poisoner.

The Blandy home in Hart Street, Henley was later demolished and another house built on the site, but sometimes Mary's ghost is said to stand beneath an old mulberry tree at the end of the garden.

In 1969, she made a dramatic appearance at the Kenton Theatre in Henley. *The Hanging Wood*, a play by Joan Morgan, based on Mary Blandy's story, was in rehearsal at the theatre when people began to notice various odd happenings. Doors would open by themselves, then slam shut suddenly, and lights came on and off without human intervention. Then the cast noticed the figure of a woman standing at the back of the theatre watching the rehearsals. Whenever anyone approached her, however, she faded away into the shadows and was gone. Miss Morgan remembered that some years before, when a dramatised version of Mary Blandy's trial was performed at Henley Town Hall, a similar figure had been seen at the back of the hall while they were rehearsing.

Was it the ghost of Mary Blandy herself? Naturally, members of the cast thought so, and one evening as they sat drinking coffee and talking about her, something happened to convince any sceptics. Someone had placed a cup on the floor and, as the cast watched in amazement, it rose right up for several inches, and then was dashed down again to break into pieces.

Until recently, there was apparently no known portrait of Mary Blandy in her home town, but in 1987 the Hon Georgina Stonor discovered a print of her, which she presented to the town the following year. One must admit that, if this is a true likeness, Mary has a cool and calculating stare, and her heavily lidded eyes appear to view the world with deep suspicion. Surely a woman like that would have recognised that Cranstoun's love philtres were nothing other than the deadly poison, arsenic?

Was Mary Blandy guilty or was she innocent after all? Who can say, but it seems her spirit is still restless.

9

The Mischievous Quaker

'LOYAL and ancient' Buckingham is a charming old market town with a long history. King Alfred chose it for the county town but later it was superseded by Aylesbury, which was much better placed for the business of local government.

In 1748 Lord Cobham built the ornate, castellated building, which resembles a fairytale castle, at the foot of Market Hill, to act as a gaol in the hope of retaining the assizes, but although the shire's splendid emblem of a chained swan surmounts the clock tower of Buckingham town hall, busy, thriving Aylesbury became the seat of power.

The picturesque, half-timbered building in the High Street known as the Old Market House is one of the oldest in Buckingham, where a third of the town was destroyed by a disastrous fire in 1725. It is a bar and restaurant now, and, one winter morning in 1994, I sat drinking coffee there, looking through the diamond-paned windows towards the Old Gaol. I had come to meet Mr Georgiou, the restaurant director, to find out about the mischievous Quaker lady who was said to haunt the building.

At the time, decorating work was just being finished, so the restaurant was closed and I had the room to myself. It was very quiet and I remembered rather uneasily that sometimes the ghost was said to draw up a chair and join lone visitors.

But it was Mr Georgiou who joined me, and I soon heard that he was no stranger to the phantom presence, which lingers in what was once a merchant's house, where the present wine cellar was the scene of cock fighting, patronised by no less a personage than the Duke of Buckingham.

Upstairs, the door of Mr Georgiou's bedroom is at the end of the landing, and there is another door on the right. This is the area where he told me he has had many an encounter with the ghost.

'In the evening when I come out from my room, sometimes I see this lady coming out of the other room,' Mr Georgiou said. 'I don't see her face, she is half turned away from me as she comes out of the door and then walks ahead towards the bathroom. She is tall and graceful, wearing a long, black dress with a big collar round her neck.'

He assured me that he didn't find the apparition frightening. 'I have seen her often,' he said, 'usually about eleven o'clock at night, and she always does the same thing. We have never met face to face, she is always turned away.'

I went into the room from which the ghost emerges. It is a small storage area with a sloping ceiling and, outside, the landing curves round towards the little bathroom that Mr Georgiou uses. Although the bathroom felt comfortably warm and cosy inside, as I paused by the doorway I was conscious of a distinct chill as a prickle of icy cold ran down my spine. Was it my imagination, or was the Market House's mysterious wraith nearer than we thought?

The bathroom has two small windows set high in the wall, with curtains which Mr Georgiou never bothers to draw as it is quite impossible to overlook the room from outside. But, curiously enough, he says he often finds that the curtains have been drawn when he goes in there.

He recalled that when he first joined the company that owns the restaurant, he brought his wife to show her where he was going to work. It was a Sunday so the building was closed and as they walked round to the side where the small bathroom window is high up, overlooking the street, he happened to glance upwards. Although he knew the place was empty, to his surprise he thought he could see someone looking down from the inside.

'It was like a shadow', he said, 'and I asked my wife if she could see it, but she couldn't see anything.'

Mr Georgiou has only encountered the phantom Quaker upstairs, never in the restaurant. But when I asked the secretary if she had ever seen the ghost, she told me that sometimes, on her own in the building, she has come downstairs into the restaurant and glimpsed something out of the corner of her eye. But when she turns to look, there is nothing.

The adjoining house once belonged to the same company, and Mr Georgiou showed me an annexe in the next door garden where he used to sleep. 'When I went to bed at night sometimes I would hear footsteps. They were right in the same room with me,' he told me. 'I used to lie there waiting for the next step as they came closer, but as soon as I put the light on they stopped, and the room was empty.'

He said that once he fitted up a room in the annexe for a chambermaid to occupy, but she came rushing out, saying 'I can't sleep there, it makes me feel terrible.'

A chef who used to work in the building told Mr Georgiou that at one time there was a bell hanging at the foot of the staircase, and sometimes, after the restaurant was closed and he was alone in the kitchen clearing up, he would hear it ringing. But when he went to see, there was never anyone there.

There is another story which illustrates the ghost's reputation for mischievous behaviour. When gentlemen are in the gents' loo, she has been known to tap them on the shoulder so that they turn round, with disastrous results to the fronts of their trousers!

So what is she doing in the Old Market House, this Quaker lady with a lively sense of humour? Mr Georgiou said he had heard there may once have been a Quaker meeting house and a burial ground at the back.

Mr Desmond Bonner, the author of *Buckingham, A History of a Country Market Town*, was able to clarify the situation. He confirmed that the site of a disused Quaker meeting house was at the back of the Old Market House, and that there had been a graveyard there, where burials probably took place about 200 years ago. This is commemorated by the name Quaker Orchard.

Buckinghamshire has well-known connections with the Quakers and William Penn, founder of Pennsylvania, is buried at Jordans with his two wives and ten of his sixteen children. Perhaps the Old Market House's mischievous ghost found her fellow Quakers too grave and solemn for her liking. And maybe some misdemeanour has kept her spirit earthbound for so many years. Shall we ever know her story?

10

The Hell-Fire Club

A GROUP of white robed monks were celebrating mass in the ruined chapel of Medmenham Abbey, the light from flickering black candles falling on faces well known in the public life of 18th-century London.

For these were men powerful in the Government of the day, but on this night, as on many others, they were the decadent, devil-worshipping Friars of St Francis, enjoying one of their habitual evenings of blasphemy and debauchery.

On this particular occasion, as their abbot called upon their satanic master to honour his disciples with his presence, there was an unexpected and terrifying climax to their depraved rites. The lid of a large chest in the corner was flung back with a crash, and suddenly a 'horned and sooty' being of alarming aspect was there among them. As the frightened friars scattered, the apparition, gibbering horribly, rushed between them, finally leaping right on to the back of the Earl of Sandwich.

Shouting 'It's the Devil – it is Lucifer himself,' his companions saw the Earl struggle frantically to dislodge his assailant, and finally fall to the ground.

'Spare me, gracious Devil,' he screamed, then collapsed in a dead faint, while his satanic majesty jumped triumphantly up and down on his back, emitting ear-piercing noises.

When Sir Francis Dashwood and the other men cautiously crept back into the chapel, they soon realised that the creature that had made cowards of them all was none other than a baboon. And Sir Francis's own animal at that! They had been made fools of, and the man who had arranged this little entertainment to discredit his fellow members of the Hell-Fire Club made no secret of his scorn. John Wilkes, disillusioned and disgusted with his fellow members' 'foolish and puerile antics', had dressed the club's baboon mascot in horns and a devil mask, hoping that ridicule might make the so-called disciples of Satan ashamed. But Sir Francis and his cronies were not so easily discouraged from the pleasures of drink and debauchery that they enjoyed in their infamous society.

The notorious Hell-Fire Club was founded in 1752 by Sir Francis Dashwood, a man who would one day become Chancellor of the Exchequer, and its twelve Superior members, known as the Apostles, included Lord Sandwich, First Lord of the Admiralty, George Bubb Dodington, Baron of Melcombe Regis and a cabinet minister, Thomas Potter, son of the Archbishop of Canterbury and Paymaster General, the Earl of March, the Earl of Bute, a future prime minister, John Wilkes, a crusading political writer and other rich and powerful men.

Wealthy and influential though they were, all were rakes with depraved tastes who found the ancient Cistercian monastery and chapel a perfect setting for their black magic ceremonies and drunken orgies, in which troupes of willing 'nuns' fresh from the brothels of London played a vital part.

Besides Dashwood and his twelve Apostles, there was a lesser group of twelve, the Inferiors, not privy to the rites of the Black Chapel and the more scandalous activities.

For ten years while Dashwood, Bute and Sandwich held some of the highest positions in the Government, Medmenham Abbey was the setting for the bacchanalian revels of the Hell-Fire Club. An unknown chronicler of the time wrote that 'England was run by the most notorious gang of debauchees in its social and political history. It was a Government not of sages, but of satyrs.'

John Wilkes, who years before had terrified his fellow Hell-Fire members with the baboon, wrote a savage indictment in his crusading newspaper, the *North Briton*, which thoroughly discredited them and ultimately led to the loss of their ministerial positions.

Dashwood returned to his estate at West Wycombe, where the church he rebuilt is topped by a great golden ball, visible for miles. He and Paul Whitehead, the former club steward, decided that they had the perfect setting for a new home for the Hell-Fire Club on Dashwood's own doorstep. The labyrinth of chalk caves in the hill opposite his park became the new meeting place for the brotherhood, but the ageing members had lost some of their taste for drunken orgies and eventually even Dashwood was glad to see the end of his notorious club. Despite his earlier disgrace, King George III made him Lord le Dispenser, and premier baron of England.

In 1774, Dashwood's old friend Paul Whitehead fell ill, and died. It was his wish that after death his heart should be embalmed and presented to Francis Dashwood, who had it put in a marble urn in his mausoleum with appropriate ceremony.

But that was not the last of Paul Whitehead. His ghost began to appear in the grounds of West

Wycombe park, apparently looking for his friend. This phenomenon was particularly disturbing in 1781, when the apparition was frequently seen waving and beckoning as it slipped in and out of the trees.

Dashwood's sister, Lady Austin, wrote to a friend, 'There are few, if any, of his lordship's numerous household who have not likewise seen him (the ghost) sometimes in the Park, sometimes in the garden, as well as in the house by day and night.'

Sir Francis became ill but, indomitable to the last, he planned a trip to Italy and even had his bags packed in readiness when death claimed him on 11th December 1781, aged 73. And after that the ghost of Paul Whitehead no longer haunted West Wycombe Park.

Another echo of the bad old days of the Hell-Fire Club does, however, persist. It is said that on wild, wintry February nights the ghost of a beautiful young lady appears in West Wycombe. Her story is that one night she was driving home in her coach when she realised that she was being followed by a conveyance occupied by a bawdy party of the notorious Friars of the Hell-Fire Club. She knew enough of their evil reputation to urge her coachman to drive on as fast as possible, but by mistake they took a wrong turning in Cressex Lane, and ended up in the pond, with fatal results.

There is also a phantom lady, in a light blue or grey gown, seen in the summertime dusk on the bank of the Thames within yards of Medmenham Abbey, apparently searching for something.

The Hell-Fire Caves at West Wycombe are now open to the public and visitors are free to explore the network of caves and passageways tunnelled into the chalk. Scenes with models of the members of Francis

Dashwood's infamous Hell-Fire club are depicted to help visitors imagine the decadent activities which once took place there.

As one walks through those claustrophobic passages with their oppressive atmosphere, one may wonder uneasily whether those 18th-century dabblers in the occult could perhaps have left some paranormal traces behind. It has been said that there is a distinctly creepy atmosphere, with one sensitive clergyman insisting that he was aware of an evil influence.

While I was researching this book I heard about the uncanny experience of a young girl who recently visited the caves with a party of friends.

As they wandered round exploring the area, the girl realised that she had become separated from the rest of her party. She continued down one of the tunnels expecting to catch up with them, but on going deeper and deeper, there was no sign of anyone else and she began to feel lost and frightened. There were lights so that she could see her way, but when she neither saw or heard any other people, she thought that the best thing to do was to turn back and retrace her steps.

The young girl turned round and began to go back the way she had come, but suddenly she was aware that the atmosphere had changed, and had become extremely cold. Now more than ever anxious to meet up with her friends she hurried along, but suddenly realised that there was someone following a little way behind her. Looking back she could see that it was a man in curiously old-fashioned clothing. She felt that there was nothing threatening or alarming about the figure, and as she stopped and turned to face him, he too, stopped and stood looking at her for what seemed a long time, but then he suddenly disappeared!

It was then that fear overcame her and she ran as fast as she could down the passage until at last she could see the main party of visitors passing through the caves, and thankfully rejoined her friends.

West Wycombe has another well-known haunting which had its beginning in the caves there. But that is another story.

11

The White Lady of West Wycombe

WHEN teenage Susan was the prettiest waitress at the George and Dragon inn some 200 years ago, she little thought as she tossed her blonde hair and flirted with her many admirers that it was her tragic fate to become the famous White Lady of the West Wycombe hostelry.

Her beauty attracted the eye of many of the locals, but Susan, usually known as Sukie, had no desire to throw herself away on some impecunious farmhand. Sukie had ambitions to better herself, and when a handsome, well-dressed stranger arrived at the inn one day, she hurried forward to serve him. She could see at once that he was charmed by her looks, and his sophisticated manner and light-hearted compliments set her all of a flutter, so much so that when she served his treacle pudding, she accidentally put her thumb in the pastry. She flushed with embarrassment at her own clumsiness, but the young man teased her good-naturedly and they were soon laughing together.

The stranger's elegant clothes and handsome thoroughbred horse quite turned the impressionable young girl's head, and before long Sukie believed herself to be in love. And when he returned to the inn again and again, it was not difficult to convince herself that he felt the same. In her romantic imagination he was a young nobleman who, before long, would declare his passion and whisk her off to become his lady, although her fellow servants believed the mysterious stranger was more likely to be a highwayman.

The stars in her eyes blinded Sukie to the disgruntled stares of three of her local admirers. Realising that none of them had the slightest chance of winning her now, the trio joined forces to plot a cruel trick to bring her down to earth.

When a message arrived for her one day, supposedly from her handsome stranger, it was all Sukie's romantic heart could have desired. She was to meet him the next night in the chalk caves close by, and to wear a white gown.

What could this mean but an elopement? Every spare moment she had was spent stitching herself a wedding dress, and heart beating fast, Sukie, her white dress gleaming in the light of her lantern, tripped happily into the caves to meet her lover. But it was not her mysterious stranger who emerged from the shadows but three local yokels she knew only too well, all laughing raucously at her anger and disappointment.

In a fury Sukie picked up every lump of chalk she could find and pelted her tormentors, but still laughing they caught hold of her and spun her round and round until she was dizzy. She lost her balance on the slippery floor and fell, hitting her head hard against the wall. As she lay unconscious, the three young men realised that their joke had gone disastrously wrong. They picked up her limp body and carried her back to the inn, where they laid her on her bed and crept away, hoping that she would soon recover.

But next morning, her fellow servants found the

beautiful young serving wench dead and, to do them credit, the three lads confessed to what had happened. But the local Sheriff decided that Sukie had not died from the physical injury she had suffered, but from humiliation and a broken heart.

Poor Sukie. Did her well-dressed admirer hear what had happened to her? Perhaps he did, as he was never again seen at the George and Dragon.

It was only a few days after Sukie's funeral that strange things began to happen at the inn, and none of the maids would sleep in what had been her bedroom. It became unnaturally cold at times, and sometimes a white figure appeared in the passages or was seen drifting through the garden.

Since then, the White Lady has haunted the inn, and one very interesting account appeared in the *Reader's Digest* for October 1967. An American writer, Jhan Robbins, went to stay at the George and Dragon, and when he noticed that there was a hole in the pastry of his treacle pudding, as if someone had accidentally put their thumb in it, the staff explained that this was one of Sukie's little tricks, a sure sign that her ghost was about.

Intrigued, Robbins asked if he could sleep in the haunted bedroom, and the landlord rather unwillingly agreed. 'You can, if you really want to,' he said, 'but we've got other rooms. My dog won't go in there.' And he warned the American that people who had stayed in the room had spent a very disturbed night.

Robbins settled down in the haunted bedroom that night, and at first he found everything disappointingly normal. It wasn't long before he dropped off to sleep but he woke with a start, feeling as if an ice cold hand had been placed on his forehead. Someone must be playing a joke on him he thought, but when he put on the light, the room was empty. This happened several times. Whenever he turned off the light, he felt icy cold fingers touching his face, but as soon as he switched on the bulb over the bed, there was nothing to be seen.

Then he noticed a pinpoint of light near the bedroom door. As he watched, it began to grow, until it was about two ft in diameter and almost four ft high. He described it as having an 'opaque, pearly quality', but it vanished when the room was lit.

He found, however, that as soon as he switched the light off again, the apparition was there. So, plucking up all the courage he could muster, he got out of bed and walked towards it. But as he reached it he experienced a feeling of the most intense cold and had difficulty breathing. His limbs were heavy and he felt so strange that he wondered if he was having a heart attack. In addition to his physical sensations, he was overwhelmed by a feeling of depression as he thought sadly of poor Sukie's humiliation and disappointment, with no one to protect her dignity on the night she met her tragic death. But his sadness turned to alarm as the luminous shape surged towards him, and he leapt back into the bed, and switched on the light. And as before, to his immense relief, the apparition had gone.

The widow of a previous landlord once encountered the ghost, although, at first glance, she simply thought it was one of the kitchen staff. She had gone up to the girl's bedroom to look for her, and when she opened the door, saw someone sitting hunched-up, gazing miserably into the fireplace. But before she could ask what was the matter, the figure slowly melted away!

Sometimes various articles have disappeared and

turned up later in unexpected places. Is it Sukie playing mischievous tricks? Perhaps not, as the White Lady does not have the George and Dragon entirely to herself, ghost-wise. In the Journal of the Royal Society of Arts, H. Harman wrote in 1933, 'It is the age-old staircase that is supposed to be haunted . . . footsteps could be heard distinctly coming down the stairs night after night reputed to be those of a man who, by tradition, was murdered in one of the rooms in the dim past.'

When I visited the ancient four-storey inn while researching this book, it was in the middle of extensive reconstruction and redecorating. The landlord said that Sukie had not put in an appearance during the five or six years he had been there. 'But perhaps she'll come back when the renovations are finished,' he said.

Time after time it seems that there is nothing like building work to awaken the curiosity of dormant spirits so, who knows, maybe the George and Dragon has not yet seen the last of its White Lady.

12

No Laughing Matter

IT is not often that a man is murdered because of a misplaced sense of humour, but a market gardener called Noble Edden, whose ghost haunts the crossroads where the Aylesbury and Haddenham roads intersect near Thame, undoubtedly met his untimely death because he laughed at the wrong time in the wrong place.

His story was told in *Sketches of the Bucks Countryside* by H. Harman, who had it from a 90 year old local man, who in turn had heard his grandfather and others talking about it when he was young.

In the early 19th century sheep stealing was still a crime, with terrible consequences for any miscreant caught in the act. It was because of this that in 1828 Edden did not immediately report two local bad lots, Messrs Sewell and Tylor, when he happened to see them helping themselves to a sheep from a neighbouring farmer's flock. No doubt he might have felt less compassionate if the thieves had visited his own property at Crendon, but, as it was, he knew that the penalty for sheep stealing was transportation, or even death, and so he decided to say nothing when enquiries were made later.

But Noble Edden was not about to let the two thieves get away with it scot free. The next time he saw them, on impulse he baa-ed like a sheep. And the next time. It amused him to see the red faces and furious reactions of Sewell and Tylor, who realised at once that they were totally dependent on Edden's silence.

And there was only one way they could make sure of this. From that moment on, his life was in danger. Perhaps Edden had a presentiment that his joke had misfired, for one night, returning from Aylesbury market, he told a man travelling with him that he feared something bad was about to happen to him. His friend offered to continue all the way home with him, but Edden laughed it off and set his passenger down at Hudnall Farm as usual.

But the premonition was all too true. Sewell and Tylor were lying in wait for him, and as he reached Anxey Bushes, he was set upon and murdered.

Meanwhile, Mrs Edden was peacefully ironing in her farmhouse kitchen, expecting that her husband would soon be home from market, so it was with a great sense of shock that she suddenly saw a terrifying vision appear in front of her. There was her husband on his way home and, unknown to him, another man carrying a heavy stone hammer appeared behind him. She gasped in horror as the man, whom she recognised as Tylor, raised the hammer and struck her husband down.

As the terrifying sight disappeared, poor Mrs Edden screamed, and rushed to call for help, and when her neighbours came running, they all set out at once to look for her husband. Noble's body was soon discovered, too late to save him. He had been savagely bludgeoned to death, just as her vision had foretold. But although Noble's wife was convinced that she knew that her husband had been murdered by Tylor, just as certainly as if she had been there, a vision was not considered to be evidence. The verdict at the inquest was 'Murder by person or persons unknown'.

In those days it was believed that a murdered body would bleed at the touch of its killer and, in an attempt to prove his guilt, Mrs Edden demanded that Tylor should come and touch her husband's corpse. Not surprisingly, he could not be persuaded to do it.

Not long afterwards Edden's son was driving home when two men waylaid him. They threatened to do the same to him as they had done to his father, but he managed to beat them off and escape. Although it was dark, he was convinced he recognised their voices as Sewell and Tylor.

When, a few months later, Sewell was imprisoned for a minor offence, he hinted that Tylor was implicated in Edden's murder. Tylor was arrested, but he was soon released for absence of proof and, with an amazing lack of discretion, he expressed his jubilation by adorning his hat and coat with coloured ribbons and dancing around outside the houses of people who had given evidence against him.

But Sewell was an incorrigible rogue, and shortly after his release from prison he was back again for stealing hens. This time he was given a sentence of 14 years transportation and, in an attempt to reduce it, he went into more convincing detail about the murder. He divulged that he had been there and had actually seen Tylor kill Edden with a stone hammer. The result was that this time both he and the partner he had betrayed were charged and found guilty.

On 8th March 1830 a huge crowd of 5,000 people gathered outside Aylesbury Prison to see Sewell and Tylor pay the ultimate penalty for the murder of Noble Edden. To the last, Tylor swore that he was innocent, but in the light of Mrs Edden's vision and his partner's evidence, there were few to believe him.

It seems sad that the earthbound spirit of the victim should linger at the scene of the crime, but rumour has it that should you encounter Noble Edden's apparition at the crossroads where the Aylesbury and Haddenham roads meet, it is a sign of good luck. Even if he says 'Baaaa'!

13

Disraeli at Hughenden

THE primroses were out the day I went to Hughenden. These 'Ambassadors of Spring', as Disraeli called them, were his favourite flower, or so he told Queen Victoria. She often sent him bunches of them gathered in the woods at Osborne, and they would be proudly displayed on the table at dinner as he told his guests that they had arrived that morning, gathered by the Queen's own hands.

When Disraeli was elected as Member for Buckinghamshire in 1847 he felt the time had come to own a country estate. Hughenden Manor was on the market for £35,000 and, despite his financial difficulties, Disraeli was determined that it should be his. Without a loan of £25,000 from Lord George Bentinck and his brothers, the purchase would have been impossible, but at last it was accomplished and Disraeli triumphantly told Mary Anne, his wife, that now she was 'the Lady of Hughenden'. The house stands high, with splendid vistas of the rolling Buckinghamshire countryside and magnificent beechwoods, and the Disraelis were delighted with their new home, escaping there from London whenever they could.

Dizzy loved trees and he and Mary Anne planted many themselves, and in his will he specified that no trees on the estate should be cut down. Mary Anne designed a 'German forest', dark with yew trees, and adorned the terrace, where peacocks strutted, with handsome containers of geraniums and agapanthus, and a pair of swans, Hero and Leander, appeared on the lake. No wonder Disraeli once wrote 'I can't tear myself away from this place'.

As time and money permitted, the Disraelis reconstructed and embellished Hughenden inside and out, changing its appearance from the simple white-painted Georgian house it was when they bought it, to mid-Victorian Gothic. The house, now a National Trust property, still contains much of their furniture and pictures, and a library full of Disraeli's books, which were his great passion.

Mary Anne was a rich widow, twelve years the senior of this complex and charismatic man but although contemporary accounts portray her as a figure of fun, with her increasingly eccentric taste and inconsequential chatter, they were completely devoted.

'Dizzy married me for my money,' she would say frankly, 'but if he had the chance again, he would marry me for love.'

And to him she was 'the most cheerful and the most courageous woman I ever knew.'

Just inside the entrance of the house is a poignant reminder of her courage. Attached to the wall is what is described as 'The side of Lord Beaconsfield's coach with a description of Lady Beaconsfield's devotion and heroism'. This recalls the occasion when Mary Anne was accompanying her husband to Parliament where he was to make an important speech, and she crushed her hand in the door of the coach. Despite her agony, she concealed her injury lest he should be upset before his speech, and waited until he had gone before she allowed herself to faint!

Despite three periods as Chancellor of the Exchequer, Disraeli was frequently in personal financial difficulties, although, Micawber-like, he always confidently expected something to turn up, and it often did.

An elderly Jewish widow, Mrs Brydges Willyams, had written several letters to Disraeli, which he ignored, expressing her admiration. Then in 1851 she sent one that received his full attention. She asked if Disraeli would act as her executor, and explained that, when the time came, whoever performed this duty, would also benefit considerably under her will.

Disraeli and his admirer met, and he and Mary Anne paid many visits to Torquay to see Mrs Brydges Willyams, forming a firm friendship. Presents were frequently exchanged and Disraeli wrote many of his entertaining letters to her. And, when she died in 1863, his 'kind and faithful friend' did not disappoint him. She left him around £40,000, and in return, as she had wished, her body was brought to Hughenden and buried in the Disraeli churchyard vault where he and his wife would eventually lie.

By 1867 Mary Anne was showing signs of the illness which would prove fatal, and his concern for her overshadowed the celebration when Disraeli briefly became Prime Minister in 1868. She was suffering from cancer, and despite her valiant determination to accompany him on social occasions, her health deteriorated rapidly. In her last days, Disraeli scarcely left her side, and, refusing to take to her bed, she died in her chair on Sunday the 15th December 1872, aged 80, although she had insisted to the last that she was 76.

Disraeli described his loss as 'the supreme sorrow of my life', and, speaking to a friend about his happy marriage, he said, 'Sympathy goes before beauty or talent. Sympathy – and that is what I have had!'

He had an idealised portrait of Mary Anne painted from an earlier miniature, showing a pretty woman in the bloom of youth, as he liked to picture her. This now hangs over the mantelpiece in the drawing room at Hughenden, and on the library desk is a delicate white marble representation of her small foot. From then on, his notepaper and envelopes were edged with black, some of which still lie on the desk in his simply furnished study.

But, despite his grief, Disraeli had not lost his interest in politics. His old enemy Gladstone's star was on the wane, and in 1874 Disraeli became Prime Minister for the second time, to the delight of the Faery, his name for Queen Victoria, an allusion to Spenser's *Faerie Queen*.

Theirs was indeed a special relationship. Disraeli was the complete opposite of grim, earnest Mr Gladstone, able, as Lytton Strachey wrote, to invest all the transactions of state with the charms of familiar conversation. Women had always found Disraeli exciting and romantic, and his sovereign was no exception. And he knew just what was needed to keep her happy. He admitted to Matthew Arnold 'You have heard me called a flatterer, and it is true. Everyone likes flattery, and when you come to royalty you should lay it on with a trowel.'

But under the strains of office and his full social life, Disraeli's health was causing him trouble. He suffered from asthma, bronchitis and gout, and considered resigning, but instead, after a final speech in the Commons in August 1876, he went to the Lords as the Earl of Beaconsfield.

'I am dead,' he declared, 'but dead in the Elysian Fields.'

Not so. In the demanding years ahead, he emerged triumphant as a great statesman, popular with the people, but an economic slump at home and problems abroad inspired Gladstone's rhetoric and in the election of 1880, Disraeli and his Tories suffered a shock defeat.

He retreated to Hughenden, to his trees, his books and his peacocks. He finished his novel *Endymion* and started another. But it was never to be finished. In March 1881, returning from a dinner party, he caught a chill which developed into bronchitis. The Queen filled his room with primroses and wanted to visit him but, with a flash of his old humour, he said, 'No, it is better not. She would only ask me to take a message to Albert.'

He died on the 19th April, his loss deeply felt by the public and by his sovereign, who said 'Never had I so kind and devoted a Minister, and very few such devoted friends.' A state funeral in Westminster Abbey was Gladstone's suggestion, but Disraeli had left instructions that he should be buried at Hughenden next to Mary Anne, and so he was.

For the last time Victoria sent primroses, to lie on his coffin, and later drove down to Hughenden where she spent some time alone in his study, remembering her 'Primo'. Despite the disapproval of the Church, the Queen's devotion to the memory of her husband had led to an interest in Spiritualism and, standing in that small room, just as he left it, with Disraeli's own books, his parents' portraits and the little desk he used as a schoolboy, perhaps she sensed his continuing presence.

Hughenden is a house that still retains a strong

feeling of its owner, particularly on the staircase where he arranged his 'gallery of friendship', portraits of those who had meant a great deal in his life.

Does Disraeli's spirit sometimes return to Hughenden? In Peter Underwood's book *This Haunted Isle*, he recalls a visit to the house by members of the Ghost Club. One member had wandered on ahead of the others and was in Disraeli's study by herself. She was looking at a watercolour of Windsor Castle when a movement out of the corner of her eye caused her to glance round, to find the room's owner standing there.

He seemed completely real, his appearance so distinctive with his trade mark kiss-curl on his forehead, his small goatee beard and dandified dress. He was obviously quite unaware of her, as she stood staring at him, but just then she heard the voices of her fellow members approaching. She moved to warn them but, in that moment, the apparition had vanished.

This was not the only apparent sighting of Hughenden's late owner that day. As the Ghost Club party were leaving, one of the members turned back for a last look at one of the portraits. He was on the staircase when he noticed someone retreating down the stairs towards the hall. The figure resembled Disraeli, and it was moving without a sound, but, even as he gazed, it disappeared from sight.

In Andrew Green's book *Ghosts of Today*, he mentions another visitor to Hughenden who saw the ghost of Disraeli near the staircase. 'He appeared quite normal, and at first I thought it was someone dressed up as Disraeli,' she explained. 'I smiled, and he vanished.'

Other reports mention Dizzy's apparition being

glimpsed with papers in his hand in the staircase area and, according to Antony Hippisley Coxe's *Haunted Britain*, he has been seen on a number of occasions at the foot of the cellar stairs and on the upper floors.

When I was at Hughenden I spoke to the House Steward, who was sceptical on the subject of ghosts. She said that she and her dog often walked through the house at night and had never encountered anything paranormal.

However, there was one odd thing, she told me. Sometimes in the mornings when she opens the door of the Politician's Room upstairs, there is a strong smell of perfume! This is the room where Disraeli's peer's robe, shoes and sword are on show. There is also the robe he wore as Chancellor of the Exchequer. This is believed to have descended in direct line from William Pitt, and when Gladstone succeeded him as Chancellor, Disraeli flatly refused to pass it on.

We know that Disraeli was a dandy, flamboyant in his dress, and fond of cologne, and pomade for his splendid black hair. Does he pop into the Politician's Room from time to time, leaving behind that mysterious aura of perfume?

After all, he did once say 'I can't bear to tear myself away from this place'!

14

William Loosley's Close Encounter

PEOPLE have always seen strange things in the skies, curious craft, mysterious lights, odd disc-like objects slipping through the ether like – well, like flying saucers.

When Ezekiel had his close encounter, he described wheels full of eyes piloted by cherubim. There was no one in his day to produce the rational explanations for a UFO sighting that are now trotted out, such as weather balloons, satellites, ball lightning, or the planet Venus.

And yet many who have never seen a UFO, and probably never will, like to think that we are not alone in this universe, and that our neighbours in the galaxy hop into their more technically advanced craft from time to time to pay us a visit. For some the experience is closer and more personal. Descriptions of encounters with aliens have proliferated in recent years, and are not reassuring. Because such stories are so often met with frank disbelief and suggestions of psychological instability, many a sighting must go unreported.

In Victorian times, anyone describing a meeting with machines from outer space and their occupants would certainly 'set tongues wagging', as William Loosley rightly believed. So he wrote down the details of his extraordinary experience and hid it away safely 'to bring out when I am too aged to value worldly position'. He was frankly concerned lest he should be thought 'a trifle impaired in his faculties' and incur ridicule and, worse, loss of trade, if people thought his strange adventure too absurd to be true.

William's 'Account of a meeting with Denizens of another World' never again saw the light of day in his lifetime and, after his death, his wife thought publication might harm his memory. It was not until his great-great-granddaughter Hazel forced open a small drawer wedged into the back of a desk that William's manuscript was found behind it, and eventually edited and published in 1979 with a commentary by David Langford.

William Robert Loosley was a builder, carpenter and undertaker with a prosperous business in Oxford Road, High Wycombe. He built hundreds of houses there, also schools and chapels, and did work for Benjamin Disraeli at nearby Hughenden Manor. He was married, with five children, the last, Bertha, being born just a few days after her father's strange experience.

In the early hours of the morning on 4th October 1871, William felt hot and feverish, and unable to sleep, so he went outside into the garden. It was a frosty night with a skyful of stars, and William stood shivering, thinking that the sooner he returned to his warm bed the better. And then he noticed that one of the stars was moving.

It was no shooting star. This one moved slowly, becoming brighter all the time and as it approached there was a sound like thunder. Naturally, William began to think some huge falling object might be coming straight for him, but as he stood rooted to the spot, trembling with cold and apprehension, the noise stopped, and the brilliant object hovered and began moving about 'in a wandering questing fashion', coming lower and lower over Plummers Green at Downley, now known as Plomers Green. Then suddenly the light went out and, thoroughly puzzled by the phenomenon, William Loosley went back to bed.

A few cautious enquiries at home and at work next morning revealed that no one else seemed to have seen anything. So in mid-afternoon William set off up to the wood at Downley to see if there were any clues about last night's sighting.

He began to search among the undergrowth, poking around with his walking stick without quite knowing what he expected to find. Then suddenly he saw a movement and, pushing aside the leaves with his stick, struck something hard. He saw a faceted metal object about 18 inches high, which rocked on its base as he looked at it, and a small protuberance opened like an eye, disclosing a glass lens. It was like a tiny window, and William uneasily pictured some small creature looking out at him from inside.

A second 'eye' opened, flashing a dazzling light into his own eyes, which temporarily blinded him, and then a thin rod shot out aimed at William's body. As the machine moved towards him he retreated hastily, wondering fearfully what manner of occupant could be pursuing him. But suddenly the machine stopped, and went back the way it had come, and he noticed ruts in the ground as if made by wheels.

William's curiosity overcame his fear, and he began to follow the machine, noticing that the soft ground showed these same ruts all over the woodland, crossing and re-crossing. He saw the machine pick up a small dead creature, like a rat, wrap it in some transparent material and drop it inside a compartment which opened and closed upon its trophy. But William went too close and the rod, which had a claw-like end, shot out and, much to his annoyance, grabbed his walking stick.

At a clearing in the middle of the woodland, William discovered a huge circular area where the grass was flattened, and it seemed obvious that this was where his huge 'star' of the previous night had landed, leaving behind the small machine he had encountered.

As he watched, a second, larger, machine appeared, and the original machine popped his walking stick inside it!

The small engine then startled him by zooming rapidly around him, cutting off his escape route and herding him towards its larger companion. William made a spirited dash to escape whatever was in store, and headed for the edge of the woodland. But there were yet more surprises awaiting him. There in front of him stood a man, or rather the insubstantial ghost of a man . . .

But there was something oddly familiar about this apparition, and, with a stab of fear, William realised that he was looking at a representation of himself! Summoning his courage, he reached forward to touch it but his fingers met thin air, in fact he could see his own hand through the nebulous figure.

The spectre vanished, but more strange sights followed. While the smaller machine barred his way in a menacing fashion, the captive audience of one was presented with an amazing display of lights and images in ever-changing succession, which appeared to be generated by the larger machine in an attempt to communicate. William was at a loss to understand the meaning, so he bowed politely and said, 'Sirs, your conjurer's show is all mystery to me.' It was getting late and he wanted to go. It was time to close the shop and his wife would be expecting him for dinner.

But the machines had not finished with him yet. Another lengthy kaleidescope of changing shapes and lights followed, which William found as incomprehensible as before. Then at last came something he could understand.

Pictures were projected, showing in miniature the arrival of a 'spectral engine' emitting a dazzlingly brilliant light. It was about the size of a man's head and, after it had landed, an opening appeared from which tiny images of the machines he had encountered were shown crawling down 'a kind of drawbridge'. They were the size of thimbles, from which William calculated that in reality the mother ship he had seen the previous night must be huge, possibly about 50 ft high.

The picture show continued with the departure of the mother ship, leaving the two smaller machines behind, subsequently joined by a miniature image of William himself.

His own image vanished, and the mother ship was shown returning to collect the two smaller machines.

The message was obvious but, to his dismay, yet another light show followed, as darkness fell. Poor William, exhausted by his attempts to understand the meaning of the succession of images and lights, humorously likened his experience to a frustrating conversation he once had with a Frenchman when neither could understand a word of the other's language. 'Yet when all was said and done, M'soo Crapaud doubtless wished nothing more than directions to some convenient inn, and who am I to say that the greater part of this strange discourse was not something such; asking perhaps, the shortest route to the Dog Star?'

At last, quite suddenly, the small engine moved away to the middle of the clearing, its single arm pointing straight up towards the stars which were just coming out.

William lost no time in making his escape. He fully intended to watch for the return of the parent craft, and lay awake, fully dressed, ready to walk up towards the wood, hoping for a close view of the massive sky ship. But he had miscalculated the time it would return and, earlier than he expected, he heard the thunderous noise he heard before, and saw the light slowly sinking among the trees. As he wondered whether he could reach the wood in time, the craft began to rise, disappearing into the clouds and was gone.

William Loosley wrote down his recollections, ending with a solemn declaration that the whole of his testimony was veracious, and as truthfully set down 'as one man's imperfect faculties will permit'. He went on 'If I have erred in any small way do not let my mistake stand forth to condemn the whole: already the memory begins to fade like a dream, and I have not the patience to consider more deeply, nor to read ten times through all this in search of small absurdities: for what is the whole tale of my adventure but one great absurdity, which vexatiously happens to be true?'

This curious and extraordinary account is bound to stimulate more questions than can be answered. Was William Loosley an unsung H.G. Wells or Arthur C. Clarke, writing a fictional account of bizarre phenomena from the world of his imagination? Or was High Wycombe visited by an alien spacecraft in 1871?

David Langford, who deciphered Loosley's almost illegible writing, edited the manuscript and contributed a commentary that leaves the readers to judge for themselves. And so must I.

15

Black Dogs
and Psychic Pets

FOR a nation of dog lovers, as we are said to be, it's strange that one of the most dreaded apparitions a traveller may meet on some lonely country road is a dog.

But what a dog!

This is no friendly domestic pet but a demon out of nightmares, huge, black and shaggy, sometimes headless, not only alarming to encounter, but one whose appearance is traditionally believed to be an omen of death and disaster to the terrified onlooker.

His name varies according to the part of the country he patrols. In Norfolk he is Black Shuck, from the Anglo-Saxon Scucca or Sceocca meaning Satan, a fearsome beast with glaring eyes, and as he pads along he howls horribly, his appearance foretelling death within a year. In Suffolk he is known as the Galleytrot, in the North of England he is called the Padfoot, Shriker or Trash, and in the Isle of Man he is the Mauthe Doog, who haunts Peel Castle.

Big as a calf, he passes along dark lanes, lonely field tracks and coastal paths, his huge feet making no sound. Some say, of course, that stories of Black Shuck and his like are just Scandinavian myths brought over with the Vikings, and relating to the black hound of Odin. But in country districts they are not so ready to dismiss Black Shuck for, although they may never have glimpsed so much as a whisker, like me, they know a man who has!

A pack of devil dogs accompany the horned apparition of Herne the Hunter on his midnight forays in the grounds of Windsor Castle, and on Dartmoor on a stormy night when the wind howls eerily, a traveller needs to keep a wary eye open and an ear cocked for the ravening pack of hellhounds that scour those lonely wastes with evil intent.

Buckinghamshire, too, has its black dogs, and villagers remember the phantom of a huge black animal which terrified passers-by when seen lurking beneath a tree between Skirmett and Fingest.

Another supernatural beast was often encountered by a farming family living at Stewkley. It would run beside their dogcart as they drove between Stewkley and Soulbury, always disappearing just before they reached their destination. There was nothing particularly alarming about this black dog, in fact attempts were made to stroke it, when it would immediately vanish!

There is an old story of a farmer who lived in a village close to Aylesbury and who went morning and evening to milk his cows. To reach them he had to cross a field and pass through a gap in the hedge. One night when he reached the gap, he found a large black dog standing in his way. He didn't like the look of the animal at all. It was so big and fierce that it seemed wiser to go through the gate rather than attempt to pass it, especially as he wasn't too sure that it was a real dog. He suspected that with its fiery eyes and unnatural size it could well be an evil spirit.

But night after night he was compelled to take avoiding action as every time the same dog would be there, blocking his way through the gap in the hedge.

One night as he returned from milking his herd, he was joined by a friend and, encouraged by this support, he decided that this time, if the dog was still in place, he would face up to it and drive it away.

Sure enough, the dog was there and, despite his fear, the farmer put down his pails of milk and struck out at the animal with his yoke. At that, the dog vanished but the farmer fell to the ground, senseless. He was alive when they got him home, but he remained speechless and paralysed for the rest of his life.

Some black dogs are believed to be the spirits of wrongdoers, and on the borders of Hertfordshire and Buckinghamshire, in the neighbourhood of Gubblecote Cross where a particularly black-hearted villain met his end, there is a longstanding black dog haunting.

In 1751 two old people suspected of witchcraft suffered the barbaric custom of 'swimming' in a pond at Long Marston. It was believed that a witch could not sink and John and Ruth Osborne, wrapped in sheets with their thumbs and toes tied together, were heartlessly thrown three times into the water to sink or swim. Urged on by the jeering onlookers, a sweep, Thomas Colley, the self-appointed ringleader, mercilessly poked and prodded Ruth every time she attempted to get her head above water, then dragged her across the pond repeatedly with a rope. Not surprisingly, after her long ordeal, Ruth died and her husband, similarly treated, breathed his last soon afterwards.

Well satisfied with his performance, Colley took a collection from the assembled crowd, but the law soon caught up with him. He was tried and hanged a few months later, and his body left to rot on the gibbet at Gubblecote.

The place soon acquired a sinister reputation. A black dog with burning eyes haunted the area long after the gibbet had disappeared. It was a dog no local wanted to encounter, for people believed it to be the spirit of the evil murderer, Thomas Colley.

In *English Folk and Fairy Tales* by C.S. Hartland, published in 1893, he gives the first-hand account of the village schoolmaster, who saw the animal one night as he was driving home with a companion in a gig.

'When we came near the spot where a portion of the gibbet had lately stood,' he said, 'we saw on the bank of the roadside, along which a ditch or narrow brook runs, a flame of fire as large as a man's hat. "What's that?" I exclaimed. "Hush!" said my companion, all in a tremble, and suddenly pulling in his horse, made a dead stop.

'I then saw an immense black dog lying in the road just in front of our horse, which also appeared trembling with fright. The dog was the strangest looking creature I ever beheld. He was as big as a Newfoundland, but very gaunt, shaggy, with long ears and tail, eyes like balls of fire and large, long teeth, for he opened his mouth and seemed to grin at us. He looked more like a fiend than a dog, and I trembled as much as my companion. In a few minutes the dog disappeared, seeming to vanish like a shadow, or to sink into the earth, and we drove on over the spot where he had lain.'

This alarming canine apparition, said C.S. Hartland, is occasionally still witnessed at the same place or near it.

On the other hand, ordinary domestic pets

sometimes seem possessed of a psychic sixth sense, and are apparently aware of someone or something quite invisible to their owner. A resident of High Wycombe, for example, told the local paper of several strange encounters he had while taking his mongrel, Lassie, out for a nightly stroll.

The first one was when they were walking along Totteridge Road and on into Healey Avenue in the early evening in October 1974. It was a clear, moonlit night and Lassie, who was trotting a few paces in front, off the lead, suddenly stopped and began to wag her tail as if greeting a friend. There was no one else about, but as Lassie's owner came closer he saw what appeared to be the shadow of a man, apparently bending down to stroke the dog.

'But I was the only human being present, and it was only a shadow cast on the ground,' he said. 'I called to Lassie to come to me, but she refused to obey the command. She stood still and as I strode up and pulled her away, the shadow disappeared.'

Lassie's owner found the experience decidedly uncanny and, walking off rapidly, he thought about what had happened, trying to find a reasonable explanation. He felt sure the shadow was similar to that cast by a man, but as the moon was shining in his face and the shadow was pointing towards him, it could not have been his own!

It was about a week later that he had a similar experience. It was Bonfire Night, so he took Lassie out later than usual, after the firework displays were over. This time there was no moon, but there was plenty of light from the street lamps, and yet again Lassie greeted her invisible friend with obvious pleasure.

Then, about a month later, as they passed once

again down Healey Avenue for their evening walk, Lassie began to pull on her lead and her owner let her go. She darted forward for a few yards, and this time she was greeting more than a shadow. Her owner could clearly see a grey-haired man wearing what looked like a monk's habit.

'He glided rather than walked to the dog, bent down, stroked her, then glided away and disappeared. I actually got a look at him almost close-up. He had the kindest, friendliest face I have ever seen.'

Lassie met her mysterious friend several times after that, yet again appearing just as a shadow, and her owner has since heard of other dogs who showed signs of inexplicable agitation when walking along the same stretch of road.

Nice to think that some lonely ghost's vigil was cheered by a happy encounter with a friendly dog. But who was he, and why was he lingering there night after night? Perhaps Lassie knew, but she didn't say.

16

A Miscellany of Hauntings

ONE of the most annoying things about using a public phone box is that there always seems to be someone impatiently waiting outside for you to finish. Sometimes they tap on the glass, or stamp noisily up and down to persuade you to hurry up.

All this happened to Tom, a resident of Newton Longville, not once but several times during the course of a month when he was trying to telephone his son from the call box close by St Faith's church. The odd thing was that it was always around midnight, a time when you would hardly expect a queue waiting to use the phone, and an even odder thing was that when Tom heard footsteps approaching the call box, followed by a peremptory tap on the glass, he looked round to find that there was no one outside!

The first four times Tom decided to take no notice, but on the fifth occasion while he was making his phone call, it happened again. 'I tried to ignore it,' he said, 'but a couple of sharp raps on the glass polarised my attention. Then I experienced three quite firm nudges on my shoulder. Now I make sure I phone earlier.' The fact that the phone box is outside a graveyard might discourage some people from making midnight calls. And since it is believed that the nearby manor was once a monastery, local people think that the invisible would-be caller outside the phone box may be the ghost of a monk.

'The old manor was something to do with monks in the 16th century,' says Tom. 'To get to the church they would have had to walk right past where the phone box is now. I would suggest it is one of the monks who used to walk there. I'm totally convinced this ghost exists.'

Other residents have had ghostly experiences there and have reported sensations like static electricity, rustling noises in the hedge when there appeared to be nothing there, and the sound of approaching feet made apparently by the invisible man. And dogs have been known to become agitated in the vicinity of the phone box.

Enquiries at British Telecom drew a blank. They knew nothing about the phone box being haunted. So, although Newton Longville's phantom monk seems so eager to get into the box, he doesn't seem to have managed to make his call. Yet!

Another strange story, this time from Newport Pagnell, concerns the old manual telephone exchange before it changed over to automation early in 1971. Eric, the last all-night duty telephonist at the old exchange, had several eerie experiences as he manned his switchboard during the wee small hours.

'In the dark hours before dawn, around 5 am, I suddenly heard the hurried clatter of hobnailed boots, or perhaps clogs, on the cobblestones beneath the windows, accompanied by the rapid talking of men on their way to work,' he recalled. 'But there are no cobblestones beneath the windows, and nowhere to go or to come from in this little cul-de-sac.

'By this time I was sitting upright in my easy chair, wondering if I had perhaps dozed off and dreamed it all. But no, the voices got closer. I thought, they can't really be coming up the stairs for the front door is bolted. Then the voices were in the switchroom with me. I couldn't see anybody so I thought they must be behind the screen inside the door.

'I got up to look but before I could get there the room became silent again. I looked behind the screen, but I was not quick enough, they had gone the way they came.'

Eric had this ghostly experience half a dozen times during his three-and-a-half years manning the manual exchange at night. So who were these ghostly workmen? And where were they going? It remains an unsolved mystery – or does anyone know otherwise?

Another story of disembodied sounds comes from High Wycombe station. A London employee of British Rail had been to a Christmas staff party at the Flint pub, close by High Wycombe station. In order to catch a train back to Beaconsfield, he left the party just before 11.30 pm and went over to platform 3.

It was cold and increasingly misty, and he apparently had the station to himself. Then he heard footsteps approaching. They were not on the platform, however, but scrunching along on the ballast down beside the rails. He could distinctly hear the noise passing by below him, but at that moment some other people arrived, and distracted his attention, and the noise had by then faded away.

A short time later, this man was chatting to one of the staff at High Wycombe station and happened to mention his curious experience. He was interested to find that it was not unique. Other people had noticed the same thing, and the member of the station staff mentioned an incident when he had heard footsteps outside the office, but when he looked out there was no one about. On another occasion, he had heard someone running down the platform and followed after to see what was going on, but he had reached the end of the platform to find that the unknown runner had vanished into thin air. It seemed to him that there really was something supernatural about the odd noises at the station.

In *Ghosts Over Britain*, Peter Moss mentions another kind of sound frequently heard in the RAF Sick Quarters at Bletchley some years ago. It was the unmistakable noise made by the wheels of a trolley passing through the ward during the night, and for some patients lying there, unable to sleep, there was an actual sighting of a woman in a green apron, who disappeared with her trolley through a door at the end the ward.

The Rev John Storey, who worked as a medical orderly at Bletchley from October 1953 to March 1956, said that several patients independently reported seeing the woman with the trolley. 'In my time,' he said, 'the door through which she went led to an open space, but I believe that at one time there had been another room beyond it.' Mr Storey never actually saw the apparition himself, but he did hear the trolley.

'I was in the ward as a patient at the time,' he said, 'when a noise by the sink in the corner of the ward woke me from a light sleep. I then heard the unmistakable sound of a trolley being wheeled past at the foot of my bed, but I saw nothing.' During his time at Bletchley, the apparition continued to be reported from time to time, but it is believed that the building where this happened has since been demolished.

Phone boxes, railway platforms, hospital wards, wherever next?

17

Things That Went Bump in the Night at Turville

I AM indebted to Liz Wiltshire and her collection of ghost stories from the Hambleden area, *Valley Ghosts and Legends*, for this account of her haunted childhood home, although many of the supernatural happenings in that cottage near the church made very little impression on her at the time.

Like most children, she longed to have her flesh creep at the sight of a ghost, and often gazed hopefully out of her bedroom window at night at the nearby churchyard, but no shadowy wraith or pale spectre appeared to reward her chilly vigil.

'Apart from the usual childhood fears of the dark and the feeling that someone was standing beside me when I was in bed trying to go to sleep, I have no real memories of anything odd happening in my childhood home,' says Liz. 'Evidently I am alone in this. My sister's first recollection is a hefty smack from Mother for lying, after explaining that the broken vase on the floor had "dunned itself". Of course my Mother now accepts that my poor sister had, in fact, been telling the truth.'

As time went by the cottage showed every sign of being haunted, although most of the paranormal events happened after Liz had grown up and moved away from home. In her early years it was quite common for various articles to disappear from where they should be, and turn up somewhere else, but the family took this very much for granted and accepted the obvious explanation. Someone must have absentmindedly forgotten where they had put whatever it was.

The dog behaved strangely at times too, staring menacingly at the corner where the television stood, her hackles raised. But this was not a mute protest at the quality of the programmes as, when they moved the television to another part of the room, she would still behave threateningly at times, her eyes fixed intently on the empty space where the set had been.

Liz's mother complained that her bedroom sometimes became abnormally cold for no apparent reason, and her grandmother 'absolutely hated the place', complaining that it 'smelt of death'. As soon as she arrived, she would fling open all the windows to let in the fresh air.

The other grandmother, who lived close by, usually popped over to feed the pets when the family were out, and was often greeted by a cacophony of banging doors although the house was empty. At first she would look round to make sure there was no one there, but as it went on, she decided to ignore it.

As time went by, Liz grew up and moved away from home, and her parents parted, leaving just her father and younger sister at home. Her sister told her of occasions when she was in bed at night and thought she heard her father return home from an evening out. When she called out to him, however, there was no reply and she would find she was alone in the house. At other times, she woke up with a start, hearing loud knocks on her bedroom door, but there was no one outside.

At that time Liz's sister seemed to be the focus for the succession of paranormal events. Sometimes as she lay in bed in the darkness she could hear her wardrobe rattling noisily, or the packet of biscuits on her bedside table would rustle as if someone was helping themselves, but as soon as she switched on the light the sounds abruptly stopped. She didn't find these events particularly alarming then, but afterwards when she thought about it, she did feel afraid.

One night, when she was sleeping on the sofa in the living room as a friend was using her bed, she saw a group of tiny dancing lights pass through the room from the front door to the back. And later she noticed that at times the dog's eyes appeared to be following something invisible passing through the room in the same direction.

Until then the paranormal activities at the cottage seemed fairly typical of a poltergeist, but one day something quite different happened. Liz's sister and a friend were upstairs in her room, and when he opened the door and went onto the landing he was surprised to see a girl walking down the stairs. He asked who she was, and when Liz's sister told him there was no other girl in the cottage, the colour drained from his face, and he whispered 'I've just seen a ghost!' This was the only time that an apparition appeared in the cottage, but some time later, after Liz's father remarried, they heard for the first time about a tragic occurrence which happened there at around the turn of the century.

They were told that a young epileptic girl, Daisy Sewell, lived in the cottage at that time, and one day she suffered a particularly violent fit, which caused her to fall on the open fire. She was so badly burned that she never recovered, and died soon afterwards.

According to local people, the ghost of a young girl walks through the churchyard on a path which runs close by the cottage, and, not surprisingly, Liz's family wondered if there could be a connection between Daisy Sewell, the churchyard ghost and all the mysterious paranormal happenings they had experienced. Rightly or wrongly, from then on when something odd happened, Daisy got the blame!

Some quite dramatic things occurred from time to time, as well as the occasional bumps in the night, such as the time Liz's father and his wife were wakened by a loud crash as a free-standing electric fire was apparently thrown to the bedroom floor.

One of the more pleasant aspects of a haunting can take the form of a mysterious scent, often violets or lavender, and Liz's stepmother went into her bedroom one day to find it full of the smell of an unfamiliar perfume.

But, sometime later, a different and less pleasant smell heralded one of the most distressing incidents experienced at the cottage. Before going upstairs to do some housework, Liz's stepmother had made up the living room fire, and it was while she was working in one of the bedrooms that she was alarmed to notice a strong smell of burning.

Naturally, she rushed downstairs, expecting to find that, although she was sure she had left the fire quite safe, somehow one of the logs must have fallen out on to the carpet. But to her relief, nothing had happened, and the stench of burning seemed to be confined to the stairs area. She searched everywhere, trying to find the source of the acrid burning smell, becoming more and more angry and frustrated as there appeared to be absolutely nothing to account for it. In the end, she stormed up the stairs and shouted, 'For goodness sake Daisy, I've had enough. Just go away and leave me alone!'

And she did! As far as the family by the churchyard were concerned, their supernatural visitor realised that she had outstayed her welcome, and from then on she left them in peace.

18

A Ghost
at the Pictures

THERE'S plenty of evidence that ghosts haunt
the echoing rooms of stately homes or roam the
crumbling battlements of ruined castles. But such
bleak and lonely places must seem a dismal prospect
to those more convivial spirits who prefer to make
their personal appearances in a busy inn or a popular
theatre, or even a cinema. For if, in life, they were
a keen film fan, surely an ideal haunt would be a cosy
seat in the stalls at their local picture palace.

The Chiltern Cinema at Beaconsfield opened
towards the end of 1927 and, after it had been owned
by a number of different proprietors, it was bought
in 1960 by the local council, so that it could also be
used as a theatre.

The 60s were a time when cinemas were feeling the
effect of television so the cinema was slow to make
a profit, but the then manager, Mr Walter Gay, did
his best to ensure good audiences, catering especially
for children with popular films like *Snow White*, which
brought the Disney fans over from Slough and
Uxbridge to swell his takings.

In those days youngsters could only see an 'A'
certificate film if they were accompanied by an adult.
But Mr Gay got round this restriction by reserving
an area especially for children, and he would sit there

himself with as many as could be crammed in, since fortunately the regulations didn't specify how many young people could 'accompany' one adult! So some local children were able to watch films like *The Battle of Anzio* which they would never have seen otherwise.

Mr Gay seems to have been an enterprising character, and when at about the end of 1979 there were signs that the Chiltern had acquired a ghost, local people decided that it was the former manager, making a posthumous check on his cinema. And they were probably right, as when the ghost was seen, it appeared to be a thin, grey-haired man who closely resembled him.

The cinema had recently been leased to the Plaza (Margate) Ltd, and they had put in a young lady manageress, Claire Matthews, who lived in the manager's flat above the cinema. She soon experienced all kinds of strange happenings. Various things were moved, or even smashed, and doors were slammed shut when no one was near them. The loo would flush by itself, and once a bathroom shelf which had been attached to the wall was found broken in the bath, too far away to have simply fallen in.

Claire was not alarmed by these happenings, but she noticed that the entity responsible seemed to be particularly active whenever any of her girl friends came to stay, as if it disapproved of their presence in the flat.

The cinema, too, was the target for paranormal activity. Doors which had been properly closed at night were found wide open next morning. And on one occasion, during the showing of a film, the mechanically operated curtains closed and could not be opened, and the audience's money had to be refunded. The following day, however, the curtains were once again in perfect working order. And just before the first screening of the horror film *The Exorcist*, the projectors blew!

Of course, this particular film was notorious for the number of sinister happenings which occurred while it was being made. Sets were inexplicably set on fire or flooded, and the film crew suffered illness, injuries and personal tragedies. Stars were involved in accidents and bereavements, and one actor dropped dead soon after filming his own death scene! Strange images unaccountably appeared on film, too, incurring expensive re-shooting.

So perhaps it is not quite fair to blame Walter Gay for what happened when this gruesome film came to the Chiltern.

But his ghost certainly did make a number of appearances, causing a rapid turnover in usherettes. He was sometimes seen standing on the stage, and once, noticing someone still sitting in the auditorium after everyone had gone and the manager had locked up, an usherette assumed a member of the audience had fallen asleep. She went to tell the manager, but when they came back, the figure had vanished, and they guessed it must have been Walter!

The members of the Beaconsfield Theatre Group were quite happy to see Walter in the auditorium when they performed at the Chiltern, and would call out a cheery hello to him as they arrived for rehearsal. Once they staged the play *84 Charing Cross Road*, which is, of course, set in a bookshop, and many of the books used on the set mysteriously disappeared, and were returned days later.

When I went to Beaconsfield while researching this

book, I noticed that the Chiltern, now no longer in use as a cinema, was being gutted and re-fitted for another purpose. Did they sweep the ghost away with the debris, or is he still keeping a close eye on his old premises? It would be interesting to know.

19

A Fairy
in the Night

THERE seems to be something about DIY that encourages the appearance of ghosts. Who can say why, but often when people refurbish or decorate an old building, sooner or later some long gone inhabitant arrives to inspect the changes to the home they once knew.

At least, that is what happened to Vernon Hillier and his fiancée Patricia. They had bought a 16th-century cottage at Farnham Common, and had started work modernising and redecorating it, intending to move in after their wedding. But the cottage already had an unsuspected resident, as Mrs Brenda Lewis, Mr Hillier's cousin, discovered when she called round one day. As she glanced through the kitchen window, she was surprised to see a stranger, a tall, fair-haired girl, walk through the lounge into the kitchen 'and disappear into the gloom beyond'. It was even more surprising when she found that Vernon and Patricia were working upstairs, under the impression that they were alone in the cottage.

Then a few decidedly odd things happened. A carpenter doing some work in the bathroom upstairs couldn't believe his eyes when he saw the window latch lift up by itself and the window open. And one day Vernon reached out to switch on a light, but before he could touch it, the switch went down and the light came on!

Then, after the wedding, while the Hilliers were in the kitchen after their guests had gone, the fluorescent lighting tube which had been firmly fixed in its socket for three months, suddenly jumped out and exploded on the floor at their feet, without warning.

That was startling enough but, after they returned from honeymoon, a more alarming manifestation was in store for them. One Sunday evening Vernon and Patricia were relaxing in the lounge, listening to the radio, when Patricia experienced a sudden feeling of extreme cold.

During their work on the cottage they had removed part of a wall, which left the staircase visible from the lounge, and now Pat could see a figure surrounded by a strange greyish-white light, drifting down the stairs. It appeared to be a tall girl, her long blonde hair hanging down onto her shoulders. She was dressed in a white Victorian nightdress, with a lace collar and smocking on the front, and she wore a ribbon and two rosettes in her hair and carried a candlestick.

Looking straight ahead, the ghost drifted past Oscar, their Irish setter dog, and vanished right through a brick wall. They found later that there had once been a door there.

The following day Mr Hillier made some enquiries in the village, and he found an old lady who remembered that around the turn of the century a girl had grown up at the cottage. Her name was Elsie, and she fitted the description of the Hillier's ghostly visitor to perfection. It looked as if the Hilliers had discovered the identity of their spectral visitor, but the reason for her arrival was still a complete mystery.

When Elsie made her first appearance, the Hilliers

had happened to notice that the time was 6.50 pm and a week later, when Oscar suddenly jumped up and dashed, barking furiously, at the place where Elsie had disappeared through the wall, they found it was again 6.50 pm! and, not long afterwards, the same thing happened again at exactly the same time!

Obviously Oscar was well aware of Elsie, even if she chose to remain invisible, and sometimes Pat and Vernon would notice that the dog appeared to be intently watching something unseen pass through the room, the hair rising up on his back.

The Hilliers decided that their uninvited guest was quite friendly, although she did have her antisocial moments. Now that they had made the staircase partly open-plan, as a decorative touch they arranged house plants on the ends of the exposed steps, and one day as Vernon came into the lounge, he was in time to see one of the flower pots rise up in the air and crash down on to the floor, scattering soil everywhere. He swept it up and re-potted the plant. Then, next day, they were amused to find that every plant had been watered. It looked as if Elsie was trying to make amends.

But she still continued to play childish tricks, like knocking loudly on the door and running away – at least, often they would answer the door to find no one there, although they could distinctly hear feet crunching on the gravel path.

And there were the unexplained aromas around the cottage. They noticed a strong smell of pot-pourri in the bedroom although there was none there, and, downstairs, it was rice pudding in the inglenook! If it was Elsie, she had hearty tastes, as sometimes the cottage reeked of strong ale, and at other times there was an umistakable smell of vegetables cooking.

It is some time now since the Hilliers moved away from the cottage to another area, but when I had the opportunity to talk to Mrs Hillier while researching this book, I was curious to know more about life with Elsie.

Mrs Hillier told me that although she was not really afraid of their ghost, she still remembers the uncomfortable feeling of intense cold that she experienced every time Elsie was in the vicinity. Sometimes I used to shout at her 'Go away', she said.

'My husband never actually saw her, even when we were in the same room and I was able to,' she told me. 'And the dog didn't like it at all. He used to go out and sleep in the car rather than stay indoors when she was around. Sometimes I used to wonder if I was imagining things. I kept thinking, "this can't be real". But we had people round who were psychic experts and they said there was definitely something there.

'And one day some friends called, and afterwards they said "We couldn't make you hear, but we could see somebody upstairs moving from room to room."

'Then, on one occasion, I had a seven or eight year old little girl to stay, and she came down one morning and said she had seen a fairy in the night. But, she said, she was bigger than fairies are usually supposed to be. And she described the girl just as I had seen her.'

Who can explain the coming and goings of ghosts? So often one family can occupy a house for years and nothing unusual happens at all. Then someone else moves in, and they immediately find themselves the focus of paranormal activity.

So how long did the Hilliers' ghostly lodger continue to share the cottage?

'She disappeared out of my life the night my son was born,' said Patricia Hillier, 'two years after we first moved into the cottage. I had been to the theatre, and when I got back home the lights started going on and off, and then I heard someone coming down the stairs. I was on my own, so I ran outside and waited for my husband to come home.'

And that night Patricia's baby arrived, a little earlier than expected. And that was the last the Hilliers heard of their ghost, although they lived in the cottage for 15 years altogether.

Elsie had gone as inexplicably as she had come, and there were no more fairies in the night!

20

Olney's Shades

THE delightful town of Olney, once the centre of Buckinghamshire's lace making industry, has a long and ancient history, and I went there while researching this book to visit one of its oldest inns – which is reputed to have spirits other than the bottled kind.

The Castle Inn is a small whitewashed pub at the north end of Olney and a few years ago Sylvia, the wife of the then publican, told the local newspaper, 'Far more things happen at this pub than at most pubs. I am absolutely serious that the place is haunted.'

She recalled the night when, by accident, she had switched on a gas fire without lighting it. She went to bed, leaving her cat asleep in the lounge, but later she woke suddenly with the odd sensation that something like a cat was crawling all over her. There was enough light from the street lamp outside for her to see that it wasn't her own animal. In fact, there was nothing there at all.

Puzzled, she got up and went into the gas-filled lounge to find her cat lying quite inert in front of the gas fire, and only just alive. It was a lucky escape not only for the cat, but what was it that wakened Sylvia in time? Just as a loud noise outside while we are sleeping can sometimes be incorporated into our dreams, so possibly a faint whiff of gas alerted Sylvia to the danger and her immediate concern for her pet created the impression that a cat was there on her bed.

Or was there a more supernatural explanation for the warning? One day Sylvia had the unnerving experience of seeing a ghost in the pub. It was a woman wearing black clothes reminiscent of 18th-century style, and one of her customers also saw the same figure. And once when her daughter Fiona was eight years old she came downstairs and told her mother that she had just seen a man walk through a door in the wall, a door that had been sealed off some time ago.

'And my husband Peter, who is the last person to believe in ghosts, heard someone coming down some stairs that were long since blocked off,' said Sylvia.

Their part-time barmaid also had an odd experience. She came in before opening time one evening, and went upstairs, having locked the pub door. And when she came down again she found a row of bottles lined up on the bar floor. And there was no one else in the building!

In so many cases of pub hauntings, the resident spirit plays mischievous tricks of this kind, obviously signalling 'I'm here'. But to be at the receiving end is not so funny, and when staff find themselves the target of all kinds of unpredictable happenings, it can be quite frightening.

In an attempt to get rid of whatever was haunting the Castle Inn, Sylvia called in an exorcist. 'He gathered a few of us upstairs in the lounge and said some prayers,' she said, 'and after that, all the creaks and strange noises seemed to disappear.'

But did they go for good? When I called in at the Castle Inn the present barmaid told me, 'People talk about there being a ghost here. It's supposed to be a woman. People's clothes have been found folded up and not where they left them, and things get moved around, such as vases of flowers. I haven't seen anything myself and', she laughed, 'I don't want to.'

Another man there told me that at one time he worked in the bar and lived upstairs. 'I used to have a sun bed up there, and spent some time on it when I came off duty,' he said. 'One day I was lying on it when somebody definitely tapped me on the shoulder, but when I looked round to see who it was, there was nobody there. Of course,' he added, 'I'm a sceptic.'

So why is the Castle Inn haunted? When a building is as old as this, there are usually stories of dark doings in the past that may have left some kind of supernatural heritage behind. There are local rumours that long ago there was a horrific murder in a blacksmith's in the town, and the previous landlady, Sylvia, suggested that it could have happened in the smithy which used to exist next door to the pub. The smithy is gone now, and an extension to the pub has been built where it stood, to make a games room where the local young men play pool.

According to the present barmaid, a phantom coach and horses is supposed to drive through this part of the pub once a year, but no one seemed to know the date of this remarkable happening.

I wondered if this was some kind of ghostly re-play of the arrival of a coach at the smithy in time gone by. However, Olney folklore has some dramatic stories concerning a bottomless pond called the Whirly Pit, near where the Castle Inn stands.

This pond was supposed to have an underground passage running beneath it, and there are at least two legendary tales of wild midnight rides as coaches drawn by headless horses careered through this subterranean tunnel. In one story it is the Devil himself who is the passenger, while the other concerns two people fleeing from a murder. As both their coachman and horses were headless, not surprisingly they repeatedly took the wrong turning and ended back at the Whirly Pit to drive on through the underground passage ad infinitum. Could this be the source of the Castle Inn story of the annual visit of a coach and horses?

Folklore apart, in a book called *The Town of Cowper*, which was published in 1893 and celebrates the connection with the 18th-century poet William Cowper, Thomas Wright explains that, in the deeds of the Castle Inn, neighbouring ground is called the old churchyard. This is because Olney's first church is thought to have been erected here at about the time of Canute, but when it became badly dilapidated, the present church was built at the other end of the town, on the banks of the river Ouse, in the early 14th century. However, the old graveyard continued to be used, probably until the Reformation, and there is gruesome evidence of this in the shape of human bones, which have been discovered 'in great quantities'. And, says Thomas Wright, when foundations were being excavated for some new cottages in 1881, several complete skeletons were unearthed.

With a history like this, it is not surprising that there could be a ghost story or two at the old Castle Inn.

21

They Rented a Ghost...

BECAUSE the following events have occurred in recent years, some names have been changed for the sake of privacy.

...One

ANYONE who has known the frustration of waiting on a council housing list for a home of their own will understand the delight of a young Chesham couple when they heard that at last after eight years, there was a three bedroomed house available for them.

Two days after Christmas they left their cramped one bedroomed flat and moved into their new home with their three young sons. They got busy right away, painting and decorating and turning the small modern house into the comfortable home they had wanted for so long.

It was disappointing that their eldest boy, six year old Jamie, didn't like his new home at all. It was difficult to get him to settle down to sleep there, and he started having nightmares during which he would wake screaming and run into his parents' room in the night saying he was frightened.

Ben, the baby, was just six months old, and he,

too, seemed unusually restless, often waking in the night. Only three year old Gary seemed quite happy in his new surroundings.

Then three weeks after they had moved in, Sandra, the wife, woke suddenly one night because she felt a bump at the side of the bed, and saw the curtains were moving.

'I didn't think too much of it at the time,' she said, 'but the next day the house seemed different.'

It crossed her mind, that while they were doing the decorating, she and her husband, Paul, had heard a few bumps but the house was semi-detached and the occasional noise was only to be expected. Jamie, however, still seemed nervous and unhappy. He had become very clinging, following his mother everywhere and not wanting to go to school.

And often Sandra and Paul were disturbed in the night when they felt their bed actually move beneath them. 'It shook enough to wake me up,' said Sandra. 'I would look at the baby in the carrycot in the bedroom, and he would be just lying there wide awake looking around. Sometimes when I was sitting down I felt a sensation like something touching my hair, or touching my arm. I felt as if something was going to happen.'

And sure enough, on a February day that the superstitious consider particularly unlucky – Friday the 13th – events took a really frightening turn.

Sandra was chatting to a neighbour who mentioned both that the previous occupant of the house had been a medium, and that his wife was a member of the Spiritualist church. When she heard this, Sandra decided to seek the advice of Robin Smith, the Team Rector of Great Chesham, who had married her and Paul seven years before.

Robin Smith was reassuring. It was not the first time he had heard of buildings with an unquiet atmosphere, and he suggested that he should come and bless the house. He came, and after the blessing tried to calm Sandra's fears. 'While he was there I felt easier,' she explained. 'He said things would either quieten down or we would have to take more drastic measures.'

But later that afternoon, when Sandra went up to the bathroom with Jamie, she was left in no doubt that some powerful and evil paranormal force was still present in the house. 'Suddenly I felt cold, and so frightened. I was really petrified,' she recalled. 'I grabbed hold of a cross round my neck and cried "Jesus, help me!" I felt as if I couldn't breathe.'

Sandra's mother and sister, Lynn, were at the house that afternoon, and they heard her cry out and come tumbling down the stairs. 'She came down screaming "It's got me", her eyes popping out, and she was calling out "Help me" in a man's voice,' said Lynn.

Sandra's mother didn't hesitate. She hurried the distraught girl and her three children out of the house and took them home with her. Sandra felt as if the spirit had been trying to possess her, and it was several weeks before she really recovered. Her doctor, who prescribed tranquillisers and sleeping tablets for her, advised the Housing Department that for health reasons the family should not return to live in their new home.

'At first I just thought it was the moving, and that everything had got on top of me,' said Sandra. 'I used to half believe in ghosts, but everyone has their doubts. You see something on television and think "what a load of rubbish", but you never believe it could happen to you. I believe it now.'

The local housing officer was sympathetic and, although his investigations had not been able to discover anything unusual about the property, he was able to rehouse the family.

The previous tenants of Paul and Sandra's haunted council house had lived there for nine years, but they had never had any similar experiences. And, oddly enough, they were people with a particular interest in the supernatural. 'If there was any sort of presence we would have felt it, but even if we had heard anything we would not have been worried by it,' they said. They were definite that they had never held seances in the house, and were sure that there was no way they could have caused some unquiet spirit to take up residence. And yet one had certainly turned up when Paul and Sandra moved in.

Do ghosts haunt people as well as properties? Another young couple, too, had every reason to think it could be so.

... Two

LIZ was on her own in her Victorian council house in Bletchley one summer evening. Her husband was on night shift and, after she had put her baby to bed, she was sitting watching television when she noticed something odd.

She could see what appeared to be a shadowy figure moving along the living room wall towards the door. Liz was a sensible down-to-earth person, and she didn't give the matter much consideration. She thought it must be some kind of reflection from outside, or perhaps from the television.

But the next night the same thing happened, and the next. It was a shadowy shape, which looked masculine and appeared to have short hair. Liz tried changing the lampshade, moving the mirror and rearranging the pictures, but it made no difference. The ghostly figure still continued its nightly patrol along the wall. It was beginning to make Liz feel scared and uneasy as she had to spend many evenings on her own while her husband was working.

She hadn't said anything to anyone about her unwelcome visitor, until her husband arrived home from work one day to find her obviously terrified, and then she told him all about it. He found it hard to believe that the house was haunted, until he, too, saw the mysterious figure flitting along the wall.

They decided to leave at once and stay with friends, and after they explained about the ghost to the local council, a Roman Catholic priest was called in to perform an exorcism.

Liz and her husband were present and they, too, prayed, hoping that they had now seen the last of the apparition. But exorcisms do not always have the desired effect, and that night, only a couple of hours after the ceremony, the shadowy apparition was still following its usual route just as if nothing had happened. It looked as if the ghost had no intention of leaving, but Liz and her husband did, and the sympathetic council were able to rehouse them.

As for the ghost, he was not left in possession of a useful council house for long. Another exorcism took place and, this time, it seems to have worked as the new tenant who moved in had no complaints.

... Three

NOT long after the end of the Second World War, a local paper carried the headline 'Poltergeist Activity Reported in Old Almshouse at Langley'.

During an acute housing shortage, Margaret B, her teenage daughter Rosemary, and two young sons had been given accommodation in one of a row of old almshouses close by the church. It was soon after they moved in that the family realised that there was something decidedly creepy about their new home.

One night Rosemary woke with a start to see a tall, misty figure standing near her bed. She told herself she must be dreaming, and didn't mention it to anyone. But the figure appeared again on three subsequent nights, and then one evening she and her mother both saw it downstairs.

On another occasion, when Rosemary was sleeping downstairs because one of her brothers was ill, she woke suddenly when she felt a hand touch her face, and she saw the figure standing beside the bookcase by the window. 'Whenever I have seen it, it has always been a completely dark, moonless night, and yet the figure has stood out perfectly clearly', said Rosemary.

A succession of knocking and thumping noises was heard at odd times, and in the evenings there was a sort of odd humming noise, like a top, in the sitting room. Margaret heard from neighbours that the two elderly ladies who occupied the house before them had also complained about the strange happenings.

A medium, Harold Plume, offered to help and, after holding a seance with three of his friends one night, he soon made contact with a former occupant of the house. He described her as an old lady, wearing a black shawl, with a red petticoat showing beneath her skirt. He found that the knocking that had frightened the family was apparently due to her trying to reach her money box, which she had hidden behind a corner bookcase. She seemed to be a rather irascible personality, and said that she was haunting the house because she could not understand why a young family were occupying an almshouse intended for old people. However, when Mr Plume explained that they had been homeless, her attitude changed and she said she would like to help them. Mr Plume told her that she could best assist the family by stopping her frightening activities, and, to everyone's relief, the almshouse was completely peaceful from then on.

...Four

A COUPLE of newly-weds found they had an unwelcome third sharing their 300 year old cottage at Chesham, and only a few weeks after their wedding they were already having second thoughts about their new home.

One night after they had gone to bed they were surprised to hear the clip clop of horse's hooves in the lane outside, and sounds suggesting that the rider had dismounted. Feeling curious, Bill peered out of the window, but there was nothing to be seen, so he went downstairs for a better look. No one was outside, but he found that a picture had fallen from the wall in the sitting room. Although these were all things that might have had a natural explanation, in the light of subsequent happenings Bill and Mary began to feel distinctly unwelcome in their own house.

They noticed a strange, sweet smell that seemed to infiltrate the cottage. It was particularly noticeable in the hall, and upstairs in the bedrooms, and there seemed to be nothing to account for it.

Mary woke one night and realised that part of the blanket on her husband's side was soaking wet. She woke Bill, thinking there must be a leak from the roof. They put the light on, but there was no sign of a leak, and while Bill was examining the wet blanket, it just dried in seconds as he was holding it. There was no apparent reason for it to have got wet as the cottage was not damp at all, but the same thing happened the following night, and, once again, the blanket dried in the same mysterious way.

The bed was next to an old bricked-up doorway and Bill and Mary understood that the cottage may have once been part of an inn. Were the odd happenings something to do with the building's past history? It seemed possible and, not surprisingly, the couple began to have difficulty sleeping. 'I sometimes felt I couldn't breathe,' said Mary, 'and there were times when I felt as if a sharp object was being pushed into my back. In my mind's eye I saw a dagger or a sword. I'm convinced there was a murder or suicide here once.'

They tried moving from the main bedroom to the smaller one, but things didn't improve. One night Mary woke to find two bright eyes staring at her from the landing outside the bedroom, and was terrified. 'I have never seen anything so evil. I am convinced that whatever it is wants to harm or kill me,' she said.

Although her husband had always been sceptical about ghosts until now, Mary claimed to be psychic, and she decided to try to contact the entity haunting their home by using a ouija board. But whatever responded claimed to be the spirit of a girl and warned Mary to leave the cottage as soon as possible.

'The second time we tried it,' said Mary, 'there was the sound of two people running across the main bedroom. It was so loud it shook the house. I am sure there are two spirits in the house.'

Bill and Mary made up a bed downstairs where they felt safer, and Bill placed small wooden crosses in all the rooms. They also contacted the vicar of their local church, who came to the house to pray with the couple. He later arranged an exorcism of the house, which hopefully has remained successful. That was a few years ago, and Bill and Mary have since moved. And who could blame them!

22

More Haunted Pubs

THE traditional old English inn is a warm, friendly place, often with picturesque oak beams, gleaming brasses, a crackling log fire and a long history. Coaches once drove into the cobbled yard and the steady stream of travellers may have included prisoners on their way to the scaffold, highwaymen hiding out from the law, smugglers, soldiers, priests, monks, eloping lovers, as well as ordinary folk in search of refreshment.

Small wonder then that so many pubs are haunted. Some have a romantic story like the George and Dragon at West Wycombe, or a gruesome background like Ye Old Ostrich Inn at Colnbrook. Or sometimes a tragedy long ago has left its traces. Throughout the country there are inns where some unseen entity mischievously moves things around and plays tricks on the staff and customers. Sometimes the landlord calls in an exorcist, but many pubs have no objection to a ghost which may also intrigue their customers and can provide some welcome publicity.

Buckinghamshire has its fair share of haunted hostelries. The White Hart at Chalfont St Peter has an unusual ghost, a phantom fiddler. Donald Ross was the pub's landlord in the 1920s, and, standing in front of his 16th-century inn's huge fireplace, it was his habit to give his regulars a few tunes on his violin. Sadly he was in the middle of one of his impromptu concerts when he collapsed and died.

The story goes that Ross still keeps an eye on how his pub is being run, and the sound of his fiddle is heard when he disapproves. A relief couple looked after the White Hart for a fortnight in 1989 and they were not only tormented by the sound of the ghostly violin, but also the noise of barrels apparently being rolled around in the cellar, and they left swearing never to set foot in the White Hart ever again.

In Hilary Rice's book, *Ghosts of the Chilterns and Thames Valley*, she tells another story of the White Hart. A couple who took over the pub a few years ago had a bad start when soon after they arrived their car burst into flames while parked outside, and several water pipes burst, flooding the cellar.

All kinds of small things went wrong, but they convinced themselves that there was usually a reasonable explanation. Then they began to notice footsteps on the stairs when no one was there. Their daughter was three years old at the time, and she began waking up at 4 am. Her parents woke too, as they could hear her talking, and they would find her sitting up in bed, chattering away to an invisible friend that she called John.

Four am seemed to be the witching hour, as twice the burglar alarm went off at that time, but when the landlord went down there was no one there and no sign of a break-in.

One night, he woke with the sensation that something had brushed past his face. Until then he had been sceptical about the paranormal, but when he opened his eyes he saw three figures standing by the bed. As he looked, two of them faded, but the third, a large, heavily built man, stood looking down at him before he too disappeared.

Had it been a dream? He glanced at his bedside clock, and when he found it was 4 am he suddenly felt afraid.

His wife, too, was finding it all a strain, and next time her small daughter again woke at 4 am and started talking to 'John', she rushed into the little girl's room shouting 'Leave us alone'. And surprisingly her outburst had the desired effect, and from then on they were left in peace.

Pubs change landlords quite frequently these days, and the arrival of a new tenant can sometimes be the signal for all kinds of paranormal activity to break out. Conversely, a visit to a pub with a long history of haunting can be a big disappointment when the present landlord smiles serenely and says 'Nothing's happened since I've been here.'

One couple who arrived as the new landlords at a High Wycombe pub had no reason to expect anything unusual. The previous tenants had not experienced anything supernatural at the old coaching inn, but not long after their arrival they noticed an intense feeling of cold at certain times, particularly in one upstairs room that was part of the original building.

Then one day when the landlord went into this room, he saw the indistinct figure of a woman in a long blue dress sitting in the corner. In spite of the fact that the figure was hazy, he had the impression that she had long fair hair which she was brushing, and he felt that she was aware of him, as her black eyes seemed to be following his movements.

From that first sighting, the landlord felt that the ghost was totally benevolent, and there was nothing to be afraid of. She seemed to be confined to the oldest part of the building, and although there were subsequent sightings, at other times her unseen presence was signalled by the sound of footsteps in 'her' room upstairs and sudden cold draughts, lights switching on and off and doors opening by themselves.

The two dogs at the pub had completely different reactions. One would show fear, backing away and growling at what was apparently an empty space, while the other dog would bound forward happily in a friendly greeting.

On one occasion a visitor to the pub stayed the night in the room where the ghost was sometimes seen. He had fallen asleep leaving a portable gas heater still on, close beside his bed. There could have been serious trouble if the bedclothes had caught fire, but he woke to find the heater had been turned off, although no one had entered the room. The landlord and his wife were convinced that it was thanks to their ghost that danger had been averted, and they liked to think she had appointed herself as the guardian angel of the old inn where she once lived.

In accordance with their wishes, the name of the pub has not been given.

Pub hauntings often have an obvious pattern. Rolling the heavy barrels around is a favourite activity as the landlord of the Old Bull at Fenny Stratford found a few years ago. Somehow, despite the locked cellar door, the kegs and barrels mysteriously moved in the night, and when he scattered cleaning powder all over the floor, there were no footprints!

At the Bull and Butcher pub at Turville, a succession of landlords have heard the clinking of bottles and the sound of barrels being rolled in the cellar but, on investigation, nothing has been moved.

However, on occasions the odd beer glass has shot through the room to smash on the floor, and once a liquor bottle standing on a shelf exploded into fragments.

During the 1980s the ghost of a woman was seen in the bar and upstairs in one of the bedrooms, and she was thought to be the wife of a landlord who murdered her in 1942, and then committed suicide.

At the Crown Hotel, Amersham, they have a grey lady in old-fashioned costume, and visitors' clothes and suitcases have often been moved. Sometimes the clothes are removed from the suitcase, and at other times, they are packed back! Was the grey lady once a maid at the inn, still busily carrying out her duties?

It is said that Britain is the most haunted country on earth and pubs obviously rate highly with any ghost looking for somewhere to while away a few centuries. Not every landlord welcomes his supernatural 'regular', but many appreciate that a pub with its own brand of spirits really has that little something extra!

Index